Your Life is YOUR Business

Your Life is YOUR Business

Planned Personal Change and Career Transition

Kristi Nielsen

InterACTION Publishing

Abbotsford, BC

Your Life is YOUR Business
Planned Personal Change and Career Transition
©1997 by Kristi Nielsen

For further information contact:
InterACTION Publishing
P.O. Box 272
Abbotsford, BC V2S 4N9
e-mail action@dowco.com

Cover Photography by:
Gerald A. Koehn © 1997 all rights reserved.

Canadian Cataloguing in Publication Data

Nielsen, Kristi, 1950-

Your life is your business

ISBN 0-982432-0-7
Includes index

1. Self-actualization (Psychology).   2. Career Changes
I. Title.
BF637.S4N53 1997   158.1   C97-910581-X

Some of the anecdotal illustrations in this book are true to life and are included with the permission of the persons involved. All other illustrations are composites of real situations, and any resemblance to people living or dead is coincidental.

Printed in Canada by Friesen Printers, Altona, Manitoba

To my children who have
added sunshine to my life
in even the darkest of times.

To my two cherished daughters,
Sheri and Brittany,
who have shared the triumphs of
an amazing metamorphosis.

This book is also dedicated to
all who have seen their dreams die
and desire to be revitalized;
and those who have a grand vision,
and a willingness to do what it takes
to make his or her vision a reality.

ACKNOWLEDGEMENTS

I would like to acknowledge the following people who have assisted me in the process of writing this book:

Lisa Kenney, who faithfully edited time after time to make this book grammatically correct, and free from verbosity. Her commitment to this project included working on weekends and late at night. Thanks again Lisa.

Diane Strachan, who read the manuscript numerous times from the early draft stages, until its completion. Your constant encouragement helped keep me focussed.

Doyle Clifton, Madeleine Hardin, Shirley Stone and Karl Hollander, who read the manuscript to provide feedback. Thank you for the commitment of your time, and your valuable comments.

Gerry Koehn, photographer and Scott Symmes, graphic designer for your assistance with the book cover and four posters. Your artistic abilities, patience, diligence and skill are greatly appreciated.

Sheri Nielsen, my daughter, who provided incredible support, and constant encouragement. Thank you for all the times you solved my computer problems, even when it was early in the morning, or late at night. Thanks for listening to me talk endlessly about my book.

Brittany Nielsen, my daughter, thank you for being my inspiration. Thank you for expecting high standards of work from me.

Thank you to the many people who supported, counselled, mentored, coached and inspired me through the transition in my life. Thank you for teaching me to believe in myself and for helping me find my passion. I may have remained in my stuck condition had it not been for those who challenged me to analyse my faulty paradigms. Without Arlene Dickson, Beverly Broadhurst, Dr. Richard Barwell, Dr. Guy Riekeman, Jeanne Paetkau, Jack Friesen, and a network of personal friends, I would not be where I am today. Your integrity and interest in other people set you apart as wonderful people who have greatly influenced my life. I thank my many university professors and instructors and many authors, for the role they played in changing the many faulty paradigms which had held me captive.

A special thanks to a network of friends who share in my triumphs and support the personal growth process in my life. Your willingness to listen and understand make you very special. Thanks for sharing with me the celebration of the journey called life.

TABLE OF CONTENTS

FOREWORD

This morning I read "YOUR LIFE IS YOUR BUSINESS". What an incredible way to start a day!

This book is a celebration of life. It is hard to believe that it was written by the same woman who walked into my office a few short years ago. At that time, Kristi was struggling to find some area in her life that would not only give her the strength and foundation upon which to build a future, but also to somehow break through all the misinformation, false generalizations, and erroneous beliefs that had robbed her of a sense of fulfilment. Even though she had taken a major step in breaking away, her life was controlled by fear and silent dread. I had the pleasure and challenge of working with her and watching her growth over time.

One event that stands out in my memory is when Kristi, after having enrolled at University College of the Fraser Valley and completing a set of exams with top marks, discovered that she was capable and intelligent. It was like the first gust of wind in a boat's sails, the moment of realized potential with which she seized the opportunity to courageously invest in her future.

There are several aspects of this book that I find appealing:

1. Kristi manages to express her personality throughout the chapters; therefore keeping you entertained as well as informed.

2. There are stories, anecdotes, metaphors, and poems throughout that overcome the typical dryness of most self-improvement books.

3. There is a truthfulness and astute perception of events in her life, along with the willingness to forgive herself and move on.

4. The book is structured with specific action steps to take at the end of each chapter. This reminds me of a book by Maltz called "Psychocybernetics". It was published in the 60's, and used this same method of getting the reader to implement the action suggested. A great idea is only an idea until an action gives it substance.

5. This book is not only a synopsis of other self-improvement, self-help type books, but presents a "Bigger Picture" that includes physical, social and mental aspects of life decisions.

There are other important overtones to this book as well. On the first reading, it presents itself as a guide to adults at a crisis time of life, that wonderful time when the question, "is this really all there is?" hits home. For this group it offers firstly a sense of, "wow, I'm not alone" and secondly, gives logical steps to deal with the desire to do or be more. However, this book offers more than that. Teens and adolescents should use it as a development guidebook with ongoing visitations, either in group sessions or on their own, to the "Time Out" sections. The "Baby Boomers" who had the privilege of growing up in a time of plenty are currently facing the reality of limits: limits of time (running out); money (retirement costs are more than savings); energy (I'm not invincible after all); and are just beginning to understand what the following generations have known for quite some time, that answering the question, "what are you going to do now?" is not simple or easy. The techniques needed to arrive at an answer to this question are found in this book. "YOUR LIFE IS YOUR BUSINESS" gives you the means for developing absolute standards for your future personal life philosophy, based on values, through logical, rational thought processes.

I recommend this book as a resource for personal, school and family libraries.

Congratulations Kristi for making "YOUR LIFE IS YOUR BUSINESS" a successful reality.

Dr. Richard G. Barwell

INTRODUCTION

As I approached forty, I realized my life was a dismal mess, and I could no longer live the way I had been living. At that time I owned several businesses. That part of my life was going well. Every other part of my life was totally out of control. This realization began my pursuit to turn my life around. I devoted all my time to changing my life and intentionally studied university courses to assist me in that process. As the rewards of change in my personal life increased, I was filled with a desire to assist others making the changes they desire for themselves.

The changes I made may not be the same as those you desire for yourself. The intention of this book is to show you how to explore the possibilities, acquire the skills, and create an Action Plan that will enable you to achieve meaningful changes. I have no personal agenda. It is up to you to determine the changes you wish to make.

Sometimes my philosophical viewpoint will reflect what I have come to believe. Other times it is intended to portray a wide range of possible beliefs. It is important that you develop your own philosophical viewpoint. If it differs from mine, that is healthy and to be expected. It shows you are thinking critically. The amount of benefit you can get from this book depends on your ability to relate the personal change management concepts to your own life.

We need to establish a solid foundation and framework. **SECTION I** of this book, **Changing Times and Time for Change,** will identify:

- How you can determine if you are stuck;
- The aspects of change and growth as they relate to personal development; and,
- Initial steps in achieving your full potential with the least effort.

SECTION II, Wholeness is the Sum of the Parts, provides a framework for a holistic approach to managing meaningful change. The areas identified will be the inner self, emotional self, cognitive self, social self, creative self, and physical self. The topics covered by these chapters are as follows:

- **A Spiritual Quest** - The spiritual essence of the human existence, and our innate potential for achieving excellence.
- **Emotional Energies** - Our feelings toward self, events and other people, produce energy which can enhance or hinder our progress.
- **"I Think...Therefore I Am!"** - How personal growth is influenced by our thinking patterns, education and/or knowledge.
- **Shared Meaning** - The value of meaningful relationships, and how to build and nurture them.
- **Making a Difference** - Understanding career transition and the importance of establishing a meaningful career path.
- **Beyond Mediocrity** - Experiencing optimum health and well-being requires a plan.

These chapters are designed to help the reader maintain balance in all areas of life. A person may have, for example a problem finding suitable work, but that problem is not isolated. It affects self-image, social life, relationships, and the emotional and physical well-being of that person. In building the foundation, it is necessary to understand the interconnectedness of component parts of one's life. Life is a symphony, and when one part is out of harmony all other parts are affected.

The final chapter, **Operation Excellence,** encourages you to develop an Action Plan for creating the change you want in your life. An Action Plan is like a blueprint to a builder. It provides clear direction, enabling the individual to create a finished product which will be exactly as planned. The more clearly you articulate your life plans, the more likely you are to achieve them.

It is my earnest desire that this book will assist you in creating a fulfilling and balanced life. Use a notebook to answer the questions presented to you in this book. It will provide a journal of your progress. Writing the answers increases your awareness of challenges and provides an Action Plan for future growth. I encourage you to work at your own speed, and consider this as a book which will be referred to again and again, long after you have read it. The merit of this book rests not only on my expertise in conveying these important concepts to you, but also on the degree to which you decide to become involved with implementing changes.

It may seem overwhelming at times, when you get a clear picture of how far *where you are* is from *where you want to be*. I want to assure you, the efforts are well worth it. Nothing in life can compare to the triumph and freedom which is experienced when the life you dreamed of becomes the life you are living.

Section I

Changing Times
and
Time for Change

> *"People are always blaming their circumstances for what they are. I don't believe in circumstances. The people who get on in this world are the people who get up and look for the circumstances they want, and if they can't find them, MAKE THEM."*
>
> *- George Bernard Shaw*

Lessons I Learned by Mistake

Cows in the corner of the field don't make
a good landmark.

Fearing to cross the bridge, means you will never know
what is on the other side.

Digging up a seedling to check if it's growing isn't the
way to speed up growth.

Growing garden vegetables is hard work. Stinkweed
grows without assistance, but you can't eat it.

Goats don't heel, and chasing them in fields without
fences isn't successful.

Hiding dirty pots and pans doesn't mean you get out
of scrubbing them.

If you are on a raft, don't let the paddle drift away.

Creating a book report based on reading only the
dust jacket, isn't a short cut.

Never jump on the floor of a tree fort, to check
if it's secure.

Reading only the first and last page of "How to
Assemble a Bicycle," can result in many
left over parts and no brakes.

Mistakes are learning opportunities in disguise
from which the lesson needs to be learned
without repetition.

Chapter 1

Setting the Stage

> *"Some people are thermometers - they merely register what is around them.*
> *Others, however, are thermostats - they regulate the atmosphere."*
>
> *- Aristotle*

Admitting we are Stuck

"It's not my fault. My family is dysfunctional. My parents failed to empower me. The school system did nothing to build my self-esteem. Consequently, I am unfulfilled. My behavior is a conditioned response. I did not receive unconditional love from my parents. Their co-dependent relationship, my father's autocratic parenting style, my mother's passive aggressive role modelling and unmonitored sibling rivalry have led to my dysfunctional behavioral patterns. I am a victim. I love victimhood. It provides a security blanket for me, allowing me to absolve myself of any responsibility for my actions." And so goes the description most of us provide for our behavior. Why are we where we are? What can be done about it? Are there any answers?

Sooner or later, most of us come to a time when we question the real meaning of our lives. When we stop and reflect, too many of us feel dissatisfied with the outcome of the way we are presently living. We lack the feeling of lasting satisfaction. Continuing to do the same things, in the same ways, will get the same results.

Responding to these questions personally, will determine if you are stuck in a rut:

- Is my life or situation considerably better than it was two years ago?

- If I continue doing what I am presently doing, will my life and situation improve in the next two years?

- Can I truthfully say I am happy, and feel fulfilled with my present life and situation?

- Do I have a written Vision Statement, and/or Purpose Statement for my life?

- Do I have a written plan to help me achieve my vision?

Answering NO, or NOT REALLY, to even one of these questions indicates you are stuck. When you are stuck, the present is not satisfying your expectations, and the future will only bring more of the same disappointment.

There are many factors which can contribute to the stuck state. Conditioning leads to certain responses to specific situations. The belief systems we buy into, control our actions and our actions create our future. The answer to sorting all this out is within each one of us. Each individual is the creator of his or her own future.

> *"Yesterday is already a dream, and tomorrow is only a vision; but today well-lived makes every yesterday a dream of happiness, and every tomorrow a vision of hope."*
>
> *- from the Sanskrit*

We can create using conscious competence - a state of total awareness and excellence. Or, we can create in unconscious incompetence - the state of being unaware of the influence of our beliefs, decisions, and actions on our future - and accept mediocrity. Or, we can create in a state of semi-conscious incompetence - leaving everything to chance. The semi-conscious state assumes it is good luck when things work out, and bad luck when they go wrong. Fate is omnipresent. Personal efforts are inconsequential. These beliefs lead to a barely functioning state, where the person accepts limited responsibility.

Many people drive cars in a state of semi-conscious incompetence. One time a woman drove straight into us, while we were travelling in a bright orange car. Her response was, "Sorry, I didn't see you!" How can anyone fail to see an orange car in broad daylight? Was she just unlucky, or was it lack of attention?

The answer to fulfilment is not a panacea or potion which can be administered by someone else. If we have lost awareness of our ability to create, it requires a lot of self work to reconnect with our life spirit.

It is a cyclical, multistep process. The first step is to gain awareness of the available opportunities (choices). The second step is to find the additional information needed to assist in the planning process. The third step is to determine which parts of the new information are useful to your personal plan. The fourth step is to build an Action Plan (the Life and Career Plan). The fifth step is to implement it. The sixth step is to review and revise it. This cycle needs to be repeated continuously. The synergy created by this process provides the energy needed for continued growth.

Time out:

Are you stuck? Is your life a series of accidents caused by a state of semi-conscious awareness? What are three things you wish to accomplish in the next year? If you could have (or be) anything you wanted, what would you have (or be)? What is stopping you?

Resources

It is possible to have many resources available to us and not realize it. There may be gold, oil and other precious minerals underground but until they are discovered and marketed they bring no value. Once the landowner becomes aware of the opportunities that lay hidden under the soil, it is necessary to learn how to benefit from those resources. The landowner may decide to read a book. The book may reveal the steps necessary to recover and utilize the hidden resources. However, that will not provide the person with any revenue, unless he or she develops and implements an Action Plan based on the newly acquired knowledge.

Many times there are hidden resources within our reach. Every part of creation has the innate ability to restore balance and order. From the individual cells of the organism, to the organism as a whole, there is a built-in source of knowledge which enables it to survive and thrive. For example, the self-sustaining force held within the seed of a tree, holds all the information needed to protect, nourish and allow the tree to reach its full potential. This helps the tree adapt perfectly to the environment, whether the seed is planted on a windy rock, or by a cool, still stream. These innate abilities are not reserved for plants.

Animals have the same innate potential. The herbivore doesn't wake up one day and decide it is going to eat the next lion it encounters. Wild animals procreate at the ideal time of year, and maintain a balance within their habitat. Moreover, animals develop relationships within their species and with other species in their environment. They live in groups with a definite social structure, designed to aid their survival. Animals develop a system for division of labor or for enforcing territorial rights. Without the interference of humankind, each species manages beautifully to adapt to its environment. The harmony in nature is not a synchronisity of chance.

Humans have interfered with the survival of animals. Humans have developed systems that interfere with their connection to their natural coping instincts. Our innate potential, provided by nature, can guide us to survive and thrive. Although we seldom think about it, we have the innate ability to maintain balance in every aspect of life. We create an environment for ourselves, individually and collectively. Our ability to adapt is determined by our awareness of that environment.

Humans have an additional skill that plants and animals do not have - the ability to reason. Often, reasoning interferes and hinders, rather than enhances, our ability to reach our full potential. Within the very essence of our being are many of the resources needed to assist us in achieving our full potential.

In addition to resources from within, we sometimes need tools. They may be very basic, but without them we may be incapable of moving forward. The tools may be as essential as a paddle is to a person on a raft.

My brothers and I went on rafting expeditions on the slough behind our home. Occasionally, as we laid on our stomachs peering into the water, we would accidentally knock the stick we were using for a paddle, off the raft. Saying "Oops, we lost our paddle" did not get us back to shore! Kicking our feet over the side to propel the raft toward the paddle only caused ripples, sending the paddle further from the raft. Getting the raft to shore without the paddle required more time, more effort and great inconvenience. It often meant getting into the cold water and pushing the raft to shore. Proper planning means ensuring the tools are available and that they are still within reach for later use.

Unfortunately, we often ask for help from others who we know will support our existing behavior, even when we know that behavior is harmful. It is like the smoker going to the doctor who smokes and asking, "Doctor, in your opinion is it true that cigarette smoking will shorten one's days?"

The doctor responds "It sure is. I stopped smoking for a month and every day that month was about thirty-six hours long!" We may look for affirmation, rather than confronting habits that are difficult to break.

We allow external impulses to overpower the internal impulses of our life's spirit. This leads to conditioned responses, not unlike those of Pavlov's dogs. We respond to the wrong stimuli, and for the wrong reasons. We adopt belief systems that control our lives and rob us of our full potential. Maximizing our awareness of the innate guide can restore balance to our lives.

Being in tune to the natural symphony of innate potential allows it to direct the process of creation. This enables us to effortlessly create a future corresponding to our personal intentions and aspirations, in a way that generates harmony with others.

Shifting perspectives, and adopting a proactive strategy maximizes our effectiveness. Which is more effective: to spend energy lobbying government to pass new laws for environmental protection, or to participate in educating people about cost effective, efficient ways of reducing waste and conserving energy? We need to shift from reacting to rules, or the lack of rules, to doing things *because we want to.* Extrinsic (external) motivation is temporary: intrinsic (internal) motivation is long term. When the motivation shifts, so do the results.

We may ask, "If we have the potential to create our own future and the answers make sense, why then, do we become stuck?" When we reach our late teen years, we believe ourselves to be invincible. We no longer seek, or want, the advice of parents. During the late 1960's and 1970's, the baby boomer generation found good paying jobs with little difficulty. Inflation rose to rates which fuelled the illusion that a career brought wealth and security. Along with their peers they assumed wealth, or at least an abundance of possessions, was synonymous with happiness.

As the 1980's approached, people who were ten years (or more) younger came knocking on the door of the personnel department. The jobs which once seemed secure, were now insecure. The younger generation was often more educated and ready to capitalize on the new technological changes in the workplace.

Not all the changes brought by technology were positive. Skills needed in the workplace, ways of doing business and a sudden shift in the economy hit corporations and individuals alike. There were mergers, followed by downsizing, recession, foreclosure, divorce, salary cuts, business losses, pink slips, bankruptcies. These unpleasant experiences brought many employees to the realization that the ways we were accustomed to were no longer effective.

Time out:

What changes have you responded to in the past five years? What changes may you encounter in the next five years? What changes will you initiate in the next five years? What resources are available to assist you with change. List examples of when you were aware of the answer being provided for you in a way you did not expect.

Denial

"I'm okay! So what if I am one degree off course; nobody is perfect." If I set sail, sailing eastward and strayed one degree further off course every day, in ninety days I would be sailing for a polar ice cap. I may not survive the icebergs. If I do and continue, in a year I would be right back to where I started.

Ironically, Columbus made a great discovery even though he had imcomplete information. He started out not knowing where he was going. When he arrived, he had no idea where he was! When he got back, he didn't know where he had been - and he did it with someone else's money! Well, it worked for Columbus, but it isn't likely to work for us - unless we plan to explore somewhere other than planet earth!

It is not uncommon to experience denial when there are things in our lives that are out of control and need changing. What needs to be done may be obvious. How to do it may be within our ability. The resources we need may be at our fingertips. Sometimes, the task may seem unpleasant and rather than confront the situation, we may attempt to hide it.

When I was growing up, I disliked washing dishes. Pots and pans were even worse. But worst of all was the big black cast iron frying pan. We had an old wood stove, which had been converted to natural gas. The reservoir, a compartment designed to hold a supply of hot water, was no longer needed, as we had hot running water. In the reservoir, in the oven, or behind the stove, were great places for me to hide a dirty frying pan. Long after I was asleep, my dad would come in from working and decide to make himself a bedtime snack.

After a little searching, he would find the frying pan, but do you think he washed it himself? No way. He would wake me up and make me clean it. If cleaning a frying pan is a miserable job, it is twice as bad when you are half asleep!

Procrastination is never the answer. Dirty pots and pans are harder to clean after they sit for an extra six hours. Attending to personal situations often becomes more laborious and emotionally painful when we procrastinate. Denying the need for change will never eliminate the need for change.

"Someday, I will get a degree." "I don't have time now, but I want to take a holiday." "I will start an exercise plan next Monday"...on and on goes the list of good intentions. A person who constantly procrastinates, wastes the present.

Procrastination becomes like a parasite, sucking the sustenance out of one's life purpose, leaving it empty and meaningless. Procrastination results in a loss of integrity. Commitments become empty promises, and people who live like this often look for additional unhealthy ways to escape from the miserable reality they create for themselves. It may lead to addictions to work, alcohol or the "I can't wait" syndrome.

"I can't wait until the weekend." "I can't wait until I get a new sports car." "I can't wait until I get a new job." These or similar statements are examples of living in an illusion. Focussing on a fantasy causes the present to become a vacuum in their lives. There is no pleasure in the moment because it becomes a 'necessary' evil - something that has to be endured until the magic moment of expectation arrives. This is really a dismal existence.

Procrastination occurs only because the vision of results is lacking, or because it seems like the effort exceeds the reward. It is the result of the faulty belief that "later is soon enough." Before establishing an Action Plan, it is necessary to reevaluate your beliefs and values. You must become aware of what you really believe. You must remove the barriers caused by faulty beliefs and values before your goals can be achieved.

Naturally, you want to prevent yourself from repeating painful experiences of the past. Often, attempts to set goals lead to the discovery that goal setting is not the complete answer. The power of determination is never stronger than the power of belief. You cannot achieve goals that are incongruent with your internally held beliefs.

Once you start to operate in a state of awareness, you will recognize the beliefs that hinder your progress. Present centered awareness enables you to take control of your future. Creating a meaningful future requires action in the present.

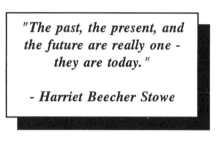

"The past, the present, and the future are really one - they are today."

- Harriet Beecher Stowe

Today is reality. Tomorrow's reality is determined by the actions, beliefs and/or values we live by today. Your vision becomes a reality with less effort, once your beliefs and values congruently support your intentions and aspirations. Life no longer seems like a constant struggle. You are engaged in the flow of creation and accomplishments are achieved with ease.

Time out:

Are you on course? Do you know where you are going and how you are going to get there? What are the beliefs and values which are hindering your progress? Is denial or procrastination hindering your progress?

Moo-ving Goal Posts

Sometimes we chase goals that are unachievable because the goal posts are not stationary. Not only is this disappointing, it is very frustrating. Measuring progress against moving or inappropriate goal posts results in a sense of failure.

When I was very young, I thought that I could find my way to my grandparents' farm by using cows in the fields as landmarks. We would turn left at the Jersey cows, right at the Herefords and then left again at the Holstiens. The Holstiens and the Jerseys were really unreliable because of their regular trips to the barn at milking time. I was not old enough to realize that the cows were moving, and I became frustrated when I could not figure out where to turn.

As I grew older, I learned to read road signs and to tell time. These were far more accurate ways of determining directions, and judging distance. This enabled me to find my way to my grandparents' farm without any problems. The goals we set for ourselves must be measurable in concrete terms.

Time out:

Identify some meaningful goal posts, and describe how you will utilize them to measure your progress in the next year. Are your goals consistent with your beliefs and values?

Faulty Perspectives

There are some perspectives that inhibit the ability to see our involvement in the creation of our future. Puritans regard life on earth as a time of testing experiences, where anything that is enjoyed must surely be sinful. Earthly suffering is not part of the Creator's plan. We have the opportunity to play an active role in creating a fulfilling life in accordance with the Creator's plan.

For the sake of philosophical argument, I challenge you to tell me the boundaries, both in terms of time and physical location, of Heaven and Hell. Some people are living in their chosen Heaven today, while others exist in their personally chosen Hell, are they not?

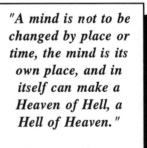

"A mind is not to be changed by place or time, the mind is its own place, and in itself can make a Heaven of Hell, a Hell of Heaven."

- John Milton

Another perspective that cheats people out of enjoying the present is - attachment to the past. The attachment may be centered around an unwillingness to let go of past failures and hurts. This leads to prolonged emotional suffering. Conversely, it may be centered on fancifully romanticizing the past. The past is gone. It is not a part of reality. Even if we attempt to be truthful in how we describe our past, it is not likely that our re-creations are very accurate.

The familiar game of gossip played by children is a good example of this lack of accuracy. Every time the story is told it changes a little. Over time it becomes more distorted. Other information becomes commingled with the facts.

Experiences are not tangible; they are at the best of times very subjective. That is not to minimize the intensity of any experience when it is occurring, it is only to say after an experience is past it cannot accurately be relived.

Think of a time when you won a prize. Your screams of excitement, the exhilaration, your pounding heart...but as much as you may want to, there is no way you can retrieve the feeling. You can attempt to convey the feeling to others, but they cannot fully experience it.

The same is true for the feelings of anguish when tragedy strikes. Afterwards, your emotions may escalate as you attempt to describe it, but it is not in any way comparable to the real experience.

Memory is easily affected by additional information. Jurors are often selected from people who have less knowledge of the case. If convincing misinformation is provided to an eyewitness, he or she may become confused about what actually happened. The testimony may be discredited if the eyewitness becomes even a little confused during cross-examination. The frequency, perceived credibility of the source of information, and believability of the information can contribute to confusion for the eyewitness.

I contend the same is true regarding our memories of past experiences. We may not intend to distort the truth. However, over time the past becomes more and more of an illusion, less and less of a reality. Our ability to recall the past is influenced by the incidents which have occurred more recently.

If new information can distort the eyewitness testimony, we can alter the impact of experiences. By adding information, we can choose to emphasize the positive aspects of even the most negative experiences. Obviously it would be beneficial to enhance memories of positive aspects and minimize negative aspects of the experience.

Initially taking a different perspective may seem difficult, then it will reach a point where the momentum builds, and results will be experienced. The positive change has a synergistic effect. When our values, beliefs, intentions and aspirations are synchromeshed, it results in a self-sustaining thrust forward. Like the intricate movements of gears in a delicate piece of machinery, every part contributes to the effectiveness of the other parts. When each part functions effectively, things we scarcely even dare to dream about can become reality with little effort.

Circumstances and challenges are not as insurmountable as they may appear. Society conditions us to believe many things are beyond our control, and that personal efforts are inconsequential. We have learned dependency. We are overly dependent on parents, family, experts, social systems, employers, and the government. Achieving satisfaction from life and solving our personal problems, is an individual responsibility - not the responsibility of society or others.

Societal conditioning and upbringing can cause us to silence the inner source of knowing. The answers lie within us. Learning to access our own innate potential can help us free ourselves when we are stuck.

> *" We are not unlike a particularly hardy crustacean. The lobster grows by developing and shedding a series of hard, protective shells. Each time it expands from within, the confining shell must be sloughed off. It is left exposed and vulnerable until, in time, a new covering grows to replace the old. With each passage...we too, must shed a protective structure. We are left exposed and vulnerable- but also yeasty and embryonic again, capable of stretching in ways we hadn't known before."*
>
> *- Gail Sheehy*

Personal growth depends on the willingness to reach down to the center of one's own being and identify what is really taking place. Our potential to grow and flourish comes from within. It is our birthright. It is our source of creation and the essence of what brought us into being. Others cannot bestow it upon you. It is not superficial and cannot come from some place, or some thing, external.

We will no longer crave or regret the past and no longer impatiently await the future, if we live to our full potential each day. The present becomes a pleasant place. It is the connection to the flow of creation. The present and future merge into a blended harmony which allows us to grow and flourish.

Time out:

List three things which you once believed that you now recognize to be ineffective. Are there other beliefs you hold which are a hindrance to your progress? What are they? How can you change them?

Chapter 2

Understanding Growth

"Youth is not entirely a time of life - it is
a state of mind. It is not wholly a
matter of ripe cheeks, red lips
or supple knees.
It is a temper of will, a quality
of the imagination, a vigor
of the emotions...Nobody grows
old by merely living a
number of years. People grow old
by deserting their ideals... "

-Douglas MacArthur

Growth: A Cyclical Process

When we physically reach maturity, the growth of new cells continues. It is a process of rebirth. The renewal and replacement of the old, with new cells is necessary to sustain the organism. Without growth, decay begins to set in, which leads to death. Allowing the old cells to be rejuvenated enables the mature organism to continue its place in the cycle of life.

While lack of personal growth may not lead to physical death, it certainly leads to stagnation. There are many people who are physically living, but are dead emotionally, spiritually and socially.

Nature is filled with metaphors which can help us to understand the process of growth and re-creation. Observing the growth cycle of the tree provides a metaphorical comparison that is helpful in understanding personal growth.

Letting Go

A small sapling grows and develops into a mature tree through a process that allows parts, once valuable in the growth process, to become dormant. The cycle of life passes to newly generated parts. While certain experiences are essential to who we are today, they become redundant and do not form a part of our continued growth. We must let them become dormant, so that new growth can continue.

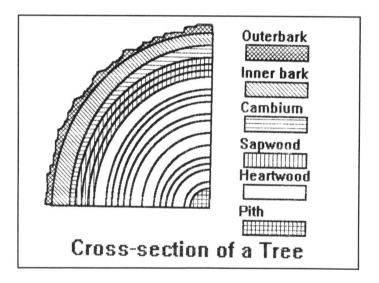

The tree provides an excellent example of growth with the least effort. The tree allows the parts of the past to become dormant, allowing for the efficient use of energy for new growth. The most central part of a tree is the pith. Pith cells are dormant and will be there as long as the tree is in existence. However, they are not a part of the growth at the present time. Pith can be compared to the experiences from our childhood. They will always be an integral part of us, but they are not part of the present. If we attempt to keep negative aspects of experiences alive, it will zap the strength we need to continue to grow.

Attempting to keep past hurts alive in your life results in poor growth. Lamenting about your grade three teacher, who invalidated you by criticizing your messy work in front of the whole class, is an exercise in futility. Focussing on the past takes your eyes off the goal and causes you to lose your focus.

Remember the biblical story of Lot's wife, who was told not to look back, but she still turned, and was changed into a pillar of salt (Genesis 19: 26)? Almost all of us have things in our past that could hinder our growth. However, some people overcome their tragic or difficult backgrounds, and make the choice to move forward not only to survive, but thrive. Acquiring a few life skills, and learning to understand the process of growth and change can make it easier.

In order for personal growth to occur, we need to learn to move beyond past hurts and failures. We need to be actively involved in our present growth, unencumbered by the past.

The heartwood consists of dead woody cells that surround the pith, making the tree trunk rigid and strong. It forms the core of the tree. The heartwood can be compared to our earlier adult years. Young adulthood - now there is a time when we experienced many of life's most embarrassing moments! But that is in the past - let it go.

At the core of our being are all past experiences. Just as a tree continues to grow through the drier seasons, we too grew even during the most difficult times. Letting go allows you more energy for

> *"Finish each day and be done with it. You have done what you could. Some blunders and absurdities no doubt crept in; forget them as soon as you can. Tomorrow is a new day; begin it well and serenely, and with too high a spirit to be cumbered with your old nonsense. This day is all that is good and fair. It is too dear with its hopes and invitations to waste a moment on yesterdays."*
>
> *- Ralph Waldo Emerson*

the present. Carrying forward the negative aspects of the past is very self-defeating and stifles growth.

Developing some meaningful family traditions can provide a sense of security. If these are used to celebrate and reinforce the positive aspects of the past they can be beneficial. However, dwelling in the past can be an attempt to avoid dealing with the present. Even constantly reminiscing about the 'good old days' hinders our growth. The past gives us strength for dealing with the present and can enable us to make better decisions: beyond that, it is of little value.

Time out:

Are there things you need to let go of in order to grow? Do you reminisce over the good old days and attempt to maintain things the way they used to be?

Nourishment for Future Growth

Next to the heartwood comes the sapwood. It is made up of active woody cells. These cells transport water and nutrients. As new sapwood develops, the inner sapwood rings gradually become dormant to form more heartwood. These active rings provide energy to support the present growth.

Personal growth can be stunted because of our lack of planning,

"You are as young as your faith, as old as your doubt; as young as your self-confidence, as old as your fear; as young as your hope, as old as your despair. In the central place of each heart, there is a recording chamber so long as it receives messages of beauty, hope, cheer, and courage so long are you young. When the wires are all down and your heart is covered with the snows of pessimism and the ice of cynicism, then and then only, are you grown old."

- Douglas MacArthur

and through the lack of expertise in searching out resources. Sometimes we need assistance and mentoring from others to help learn how to replace conditioned behaviors with more effective behaviors.

> *"To the extent we blame our parents we remain a child."*
>
> *- Fritz Perls*

Emotions stemming from faulty beliefs can also stunt growth. For example, we may believe we need the approval of others, and losing that approval may lead to feelings of guilt. Negative emotions such as guilt, remorse and resentment hinder progress. Removing these barriers is like removing a tree from a nursery pot, and giving it all the room it needs to grow.

Next to the outer layer of the sapwood are the cambium rings. The cambium is the active growing part of the tree. The innermost rings of the cambium produce new sapwood cells.

If our recent growth has been strong and healthy, it can generate greater numbers of healthier cells, which transport and store nutrients. Therefore the stronger the cycle is, the stronger it will continue to be.

While the inner layer of the cambium is busy producing sapwood cells, the outermost rings of the cambium produce phloem (inner bark) cells. The inner bark plays a very significant role in the healthy development of the tree, by moving the food produced by the leaves, to other parts of the tree. It transports extra food to the roots, to be stored for future use.

The inner bark is symbolic of our relationship with ourselves. We must nurture ourselves and provide ourselves with nourishment - emotionally, spiritually and physically to provide for our future growth. We must be self-serving.

The outer bark is dead. It protects the tree from fire, animals, and insects, and from damage caused by extreme temperature changes. This outer bark is like our cognitive abilities. Unlike other living organisms, we have the ability to understand abstract concepts. This can protect us from harm by our surroundings, and enable us to determine our response to the environment.

Time out:

Are you providing yourself with appropriate and adequate nourishment emotionally, spiritually and physically to sustain growth? How do you demonstrate your love for yourself?

"Treat people as if they were what they ought to be and you help them become what they are capable of being."

- Johann W. von Goethe

The Virtue of Selfishness

As contradictory as it may seem to our old ways of thinking, there is virtue in selfishness. It is the responsibility of the individual to choose conditions which will be conducive to personal growth. When we take care of our own needs first, we are more able to care for others. Frequently, we may look at others and assume they have had more opportunities than we have had, however, invariably they have only made better choices. Each time a window of opportunity opens, it only remains open for a certain length of time. The choice we make alters the opportunities which will be open to us in the future. We exercise free will whether we realize it or not.

Contrasting the Bonsai tree with the trees in a forest, garden or park, shows how growth can be hindered or allowed to occur. Bonsai is the Japanese art of tree growing which emulates the natural adversity faced by a tree on a rocky, windy cliff. The growth is controlled and prevented by manipulating the conditions. The Bonsai tree which is more than one hundred years old may be only two or three feet tall. The branches are rigid. Conversely when a tree is provided with optimum growing conditions, the branches are flexible and the tree may reach fifty feet or taller. Healthy trees have deep roots that enable them to withstand storms. Humans have the freedom to choose the environment they expose themselves to and their response to it.

"Every man is his own Pygmalion, and spends his life fashioning himself."

-I.F. Stone

Growth Potential

A Bonsai tree,
one hundred years old,
sits in a dish on the coffee table.
Cut back,
wired,
severely bent,
uprooted, roots pruned
and left exposed.
Growth prevented.
An injustice hard to explain.
Gnarled and twisted
like arthritic joints in so much pain.

Don't choose,
like the Bonsai tree,
to be restrained.
Celebrate your growth potential.
Grow like a tall, tall tree.
Planted wisely.
Flexible branches
swaying in the breeze.
Being the best that you can be.

Many of us were taught to put our significant others first, and ourselves last. Along with this comes the philosophy that we should protect them when they make mistakes. Although it may seem virtuous to put others first, we must meet our personal needs. Needy people have little to give to others. Protecting others by keeping secrets can perpetuate abusive situations and hinder growth. Secrecy and domination or manipulation often exist in tandem.

Initially, secrecy may cover small problems. It may start by one person expecting another to tell a white lie - if there is such a thing. It may escalate to cover abuse. Whether we talk about child abuse, spousal abuse, elder abuse, sexual abuse, mental abuse, financial abuse, verbal abuse or physical abuse, the one common denominator is the shroud of secrecy which is the ultimate breeding ground for all manner of sick behavior. These relationships involve a minimum of two people - the abuser and the abused. Sometimes they can include witnesses. Often the abused, or the witness, feels responsible for keeping the secret and solving the problem.

This revictimizes the victim, and absolves the oppressor of the responsibility to address the problem. Selfishness here becomes the greatest virtue. The victim must take back control, refuse the role of being a confidant, and end the victim/oppressor relationship. The victim must not accept responsibility for fixing the situation. Taking these initial steps empowers the abused person to become a victor - free to grow and thrive.

Abuse often decreases when it becomes known to others. However, in extreme cases the abuse may escalate when it is resisted or reported. This may call for temporary or permanent separation from the abuser. Time and counselling are often necessary to help the abused person deal with the past.

Once free from the abuse of others, the ultimate selfish act is the act of forgiveness. We must forgive others, no matter how deeply they have hurt us or how much they have wronged us. We do not do this because it will benefit them, but because of the benefit it will provide in ourselves. Anger and resentment hinder growth. Forgiveness allows us to let go and let the past die so we can move forward and experience growth.

Forgiveness may appear to be allowing the instigator of the abuse to win, however that isn't how it works. Do not accept responsibility for the emotional turmoil the abuser continues to suffer if the abuser is unwilling to address his or her problem. We can only be responsible for our own lives, not someone else's. When the abuser sees the victim move on, he or she has the choice of either confronting his or her own actions, or stagnating.

When we hang on to old hurts, we make them part of our present reality. If we bury our hurts without first dealing with them, they will come back to haunt us later. Therefore, it is important to deal with them as they occur. Ignoring our feelings is harmful to our physical health and psyche.

Managing old hurts steals energy which could be put to more effective use. Allowing a place for these hurts in our thoughts is like renting out space to unworthy tenants. Not only may they fail to pay the rent; they may also wreck the place. We need to look at the things we allow to take up our head space the same as we would look at renting space in a tight rental market. Only the best tenants are allowed in. The things that occupy our thoughts have a profound influence on our actions. Actions lead to outcomes.

Time out:
Are there secrets in your life that are covering up situations which are detrimental to your growth? Are there resentments and old hurts taking energy which could be put to more effective use?

Seasons of Growth and Fruitfulness

Within each of the annual growth rings, there is earlywood (light colored) and latewood (dark colored). The thickness of the growth rings indicates how fast the tree grew in that year. The amount a tree grows depends on the amount of sunlight, and rain. Our personal growth is dependent on the resources we avail ourselves of; the effectiveness of our Action Plan; and the degree to which we implement the Action Plan.

The tree develops earlywood in spring. When we gain a renewed understanding of how we can bring meaning to our lives, we experience a spurt of growth. This is often the time when we take control and develop an Action Plan. Latewood develops in the heat of summer. It is like the growth that takes place in our lives when we face challenging circumstances.

Trees in the forest are subject to the elements. When we plant a tree on our front lawn, we can control the nutrients and water supply. We have the choice of where we spend our lives. We may choose a remote rural setting or a large city; living alone, or with others. Whatever living arrangement and location you choose, remember it is a choice, and will affect your growth.

Just like the trees in the forest, it is important for us to be well rooted. The roots of a tree provide a firm support base for the trunk and the crown of the tree. The roots gather water and change the food made by the leaves from sugars to starches and store them for later use. Damaged roots affect the health of the tree. The root system could be compared to our individual values.

Our values fuel our passion and sustain our existence. They enable us to convert otherwise meaningless stimuli into something of meaning to us as individuals. The value of one thing is determined by comparing it to other things. Well-developed values come from self-examination. The more clearly we can define and articulate our personal values, the more clearly they can direct our vision and mission. They become like the strong deep roots of a healthy tree.

The part of a tree that is most visible to the observer's eye is the crown. The crown consists of leaves, branches, and fruit. The leaves are an important part of the continuous cycle of life. They breathe in carbon dioxide and absorb energy from the sun's light and heat. Using this energy source, they convert carbon dioxide into sugars by the process of photosynthesis. The health of the tree determines the health of the leaves: and the health of the leaves determines the health of the tree. It is a cyclical process.

The leaves manifest the condition of the tree's health. Leaves provide shade. The personal growth in our lives is visible to others. They can enjoy it just as, we can enjoy the shade or shelter provided by the leaves without taking anything from the tree, and without it making any difference to the tree's growth. The way we live our lives can provide comfort to others without draining any strength or energy from us.

In nature, trees shade one another from the scorching sun, and in so doing, aid one another's growth. We too can become involved in an interactive exchange of energy that provides a stimuli for growth, not only for ourselves, but also for others. The degree to which others benefit from being around a person who is truly living, rather than just existing, is dependent on the desire of the other individual to grow.

In part, we energize ourselves to grow and develop by absorbing energy from our surroundings. If we are unresponsive to the stimuli, having little desire to grow, we ignore and fail to utilize the resources around us. If we are tuned into our maximum potential, we will have a healthy appetite for stimuli that can be converted into energy. This can generate a healthy and vigorous cycle of personal growth.

A tree can be harvested and used for timber - a finite use. While a fruit bearing tree can continue to produce a renewable resource, providing nourishment for humans. If we choose to produce fruit that can be shared with others, we generate an endless cycle of usefulness for ourselves. This can provide us with a continual sense of fulfilment without draining our own energies.

Fruitfulness is similar to physical exercise. Exercise uses energy - but instead of reducing your energy level, it produces more energy. The more fruit we produce in our lives, the more energy we generate for future growth.

Before the harvest can be enjoyed, there are hours of hard work. Once, I planted a garden where there had never been a garden before. We went away for two weeks, and came back to a carpet of stinkweed. It was difficult to see the vegetable seedlings among the weeds. However, cream of stinkweed soup is by no stretch of the imagination edible! Therefore, weeding was necessary. Claiming control of your life may seem as hard as weeding that garden seemed to me at the time. However, it is well worth the effort.

We determine the kind of fruit we will produce when we develop our Action Plan. My father was fascinated with grafting. He would graft a branch from one kind of fruit tree into another, enabling him to take advantage of the strengths of both species. We can graft things into our personal plan that will enable us to be more productive, utilizing our strengths and benefitting from the strengths of others.

When you are needy, you cannot give to others. Life is not intended to be lived in neediness. Give yourself what you need to grow and you will have what you need to give to others. The Dead Sea is only dead because it takes, and it fails to give. Streams and rivers run into the Dead Sea, but there is no water running out - so it stagnates like stagnant people who take and do not give.

In nature, growth is a cycle. There is a season for new growth, a season for sustained growth, a season for fruit production and a season of temporary rest. There are seasons in our lives also. The seasons in our personal growth cycle may be longer or shorter than a season in nature.

Winter is a time of temporary rest. A time for reflecting thankfully for the harvests of the past year and to develop plans for the next year. A time to repair equipment needed for the next years' work, or a time to find new resources. It may be a time of storms.

Spring is a time of fresh hope, bringing the vibrant yellow-greens of new leaves. The warmth of spring causes bulbs to sprout out of hard soil. Blossoms on fruit trees hold the promise of a harvest. Soft and gentle rains, that cleanse away remains of the past winter, and the planting of new crops, make spring a time of renewed expectations.

Summer is a time for enjoying the beauty of growth. Summer brings the first fruits of the season, and times to be actively enjoying the pleasant weather and the beauties of nature. Summer is a busy time. The fruit bearing trees must not be neglected. They need nurturing, fertilizing, and tending. Similarly in our personal lives, we must not abandon the Action Plan just because we are busy and things seem to be going well.

Autumn brings a crispness in the air, fragrance of the pines, fruits, nuts, pumpkins and the harvest. Waving golden wheat fields on the prairies, corn in full tassel, the beauty of an unsurpassed splendor of color are part of the autumn landscape. The other day I passed a row of maple trees. Every leaf had a narrow band of brilliant red around the outside edge; the rest of each leaf was a deep green. The effect was a breathtaking magnificence. Autumn is a time of rewards.

Growth in our lives can be as refreshing as spring or fulfilling as the autumn harvest. It is only limited by our choices. The pleasure of cultivating our own growth is immensely rewarding and can be enjoyed by others around us. Just think of some acquaintance who is a real joy to be around, and I am willing to bet it won't be a person who is just allowing life to happen. Successfully living a fulfilling life is not the result of a cacophony of random acts.

Time out:

What season is it in your life right now? What is your favorite season? Why? Are you preparing for the next season? Do you have beliefs that hinder your progress? What are they? How can you change them?

Chapter 3

Understanding Change
and Choice

"The reasonable man adapts himself to the world,
the unreasonable man persists in trying to adapt
the world to himself. Therefore all progress
depends on unreasonable men. "

- George Bernard Shaw

Change, Chance or Chaos

Meredith was attracted to Ivan because he seemed to offer some stability to her chaotic life. It was 1985 when they courted. "Ivan is consistent and unchanging," Meredith said to herself, "why, I can even predict what he will wear on a date."

They married, and like a fairy tale, at first it seemed they had found true bliss. But alas, ten years rolled by, and many things Ivan did, irritated Meredith. As they prepared to go to a concert, Meredith lamented, "Do you really have to wear that suit? Why can't you dress like you did when we were dating?"

"What do you mean?" snapped Ivan, "THIS is the suit I wore when we were dating!"

Chaos is what we create when we try to prevent change. Change occurs constantly. It will occur whether we participate or ignore it. Although it is necessary for growth, not all transformation contributes to growth. Uncontrolled change can be degenerative, such as the condition of Ivan's suit.

We are reluctant to participate in change because it means confronting the unknown. The results are a new reality. We frequently assume that avoiding change offers stability. However, transformation constantly occurs, in us and around us, with or without our consent.

Some people see life as a game of chance, where there is little control over the

> *"You cannot step into the same river twice; for fresh waters are ever flowing in upon you."*
> *- Heraclitus 500 BC*

changes that occur. Was it chance that Ivan's suit was outdated? The stability Meredith once thought was a treasure now caused chaos, as she wanted more from their stagnant relationship.

Change is constant. Our involvement is the only variable. We can choose how we utilize opportunities to initiate change, and how we respond to involuntary change.

Undeniably, all change results in loss - even when the change is for the better. And loss causes pain! Ivan would mourn the loss of his old suit - even if he was given a new one. When we ignore our emotional pain, it does not go away. It will resurface, and sooner or later we have to deal with it.

Experiencing loss always involves emotions, even when it is followed by a gain. It is necessary to grieve loss before we can appreciate gain. Denying our feelings is unhealthy, emotionally and physically. Unacknowledged emotions can lead to debilitating depression.

Ivan for instance, may resentfully send his suit to the thrift store. His emotions may be intensified if Meredith sends the suit to a thrift store without his permission. He may be angry and deny that anger. We have been conditioned by our parents and our culture to believe that certain emotions are not acceptable.

Learning to deal with anger in acceptable ways can eliminate problems in the present, and in the long term. Identifying the emotions that are mingled with anger, whether they are sadness, guilt, or frustration, can allow us to avoid emotional confusion.

Blaming emotions on other individuals is harmful to both you and them. Ivan's anger may be directed toward Meredith, but it is not Meredith (the person), it is her actions which evoked the emotion. Avoiding the who-did-what-to-whom trap allows Ivan to focus on changes rather than on the issue.

Rehashing the issues repeatedly has no value. Once the issue has been identified, action has to occur. Ivan could decide to be reactive - by not going anywhere anymore if he has to dress up. Vindictive behavior, or sarcasm are irrational ways of attempting to ignore reality.

However, there is value in reassessing a situation to learn from past mistakes, and to determine more effective ways of dealing with emotions. Learn to control your emotions rather than allowing your emotions to control you. Separate your feelings from your thoughts and name your emotions. This can enable you to take a different perspective.

Often, when we allow ourselves to see the situation from various perspectives, we can identify a new way of constructing the situation. This requires objectivity. Our perception is our reality. Unwillingness to see various alternatives leads to a self-limited reality. Emotions relate to our subjective interpretation of a situation. Clear objective thinking can enable us to deal with our emotions, so we can move on to experience the gain.

Time out:

What changes have you attributed to chance? Are you creating chaos in your life or relationships because of an unwillingness to participate or initiate change?

Courage

Fear is the biggest coward of all. Fear flees instantly in the presence of courage. Numerous surveys have identified the fear of public speaking as second only to the fear of death. Yet, there is more danger involved in driving a car than in public speaking. An amateur public speaker who exemplified courage, was invited to speak at a Kinsmen Club about a topic that was intensely emotional. She accepted the invitation.

At the end of her speech, she turned her back to the audience and "mooned" them - the seam of her pants had given way from the waist to the crotch! How do you suppose such an experience would alter a person's fear of public speaking?

Negative experiences can intensify our fear. This can become a barrier if we

> *"I believe that courage is all too often mistakenly seen as the absence of fear. If you descend by rope from a cliff and are not fearful to some degree, you are either crazy or unaware. Courage is seeing your fear in a realistic perspective, defining it, considering the alternatives and choosing to function in spite of risk."*
>
> *- Leonard Zuinn*

allow it to be. Emotions can create a barrier to transition or they can be used as a catalyst for change. Feelings can provide the motivation for change, and a source of energy. It can be directed toward meaningful change, enabling us to move forward. Fear is the emotion that most often interferes with change. Separating irrational fears from legitimate fears enables us to reframe the challenge. Courage is using the energy created by fear to take action. Confronting fear, and moving on will enable us to experience new growth. Fear is a temporary loss of security.

Creating a reality based on faulty past conditioning, can be a barrier to creating a meaningful new reality. Prolonged fear can become worry. Worry zaps us of the energy required for creativity and problem-solving. Fear, allowed to escalate, can cause us to separate from reality and behave irrationally.

The ancient Chinese symbol for change is composed of two parts: danger and opportunity. There is always a moment of fear, as we let go of the known and grasp hold of the new and unknown. When the danger appears to exceed the opportunity, we are likely to resist the change. To effectively manage transition, we must learn to keep our focus clear.

Focussing only on danger will paralyze us, and focussing only on opportunity can cause us to deny our emotions. Balancing the two aspects of transition can enable us to initiate, accommodate and accept changes more readily.

What would you have done if you were the amateur speaker? Would you ever speak in public again? I will tell you what I did. Yes, (how embarrassing) it was me!

Three weeks later I was on the podium again, speaking to some of the same people. This time, it was a speech contest and I won first place. Courage replaced the fear, which could have prevented me from achieving the award! At first I wore a long skirt when I spoke in public. It took a few months before I found the courage to wear pants. But...that is okay. I have learned to laugh at my life's most embarrassing moments.

Time out:

How courageous are you? Are you allowing fear to create a barrier against change in your life? If so, what is this fear and how can you reframe it? Have you learned to laugh at past mistakes?

Resistance

Too much emphasis on the fear of change leads to resistance. Geoffrey's marriage was dysfunctional, and he knew it. He worked at his father-in-law's garage all day, and in the evening, worked for a security company. The days were long and exhausting. But "being at home is no picnic either, so I may as well work," he rationalized. His wife Belinda spent money on liquor, cigarettes, clothes, and holidays. When the credit card companies declined purchases, she threw tantrums. Geoffrey remained stuck, because he resisted and feared change.

Geoffrey had tried very hard to make his situation better, but divorce was what he feared most. He feared that if he divorced he may lose the job with his father-in-law. He may not get to see his kids. What would others think? What would his family say? Would he have to find another place to live? He felt guilty, because he had always believed that marriage should be " 'til death do us part." He put a high value on family. Geoffrey's rationalizations destroyed all his options.

Resisting change is like attempting to paddle upstream above Niagara Falls. Our comfort zone is only an illusion. Life is not static. Resistance is fighting against, or withstanding change, or the effect of change, or acting in opposition of change. There will always be a reason to avoid the unknown, if we are looking for an excuse.

Logic may be used to make a choice seem wrong. In the example of Geoffrey's dilemma, divorce may not be ideal. However, resisting divorce may have a more negative psychological impact than divorcing, and moving on with his life. Sociologists are quick to point to the ramifications of broken marriages. It is a little harder to determine the psychological consequences that keep a dysfunctional relationship together. An unhealthy relationship cannot be repaired if only one of the partners is willing to work on it.

Separating ourselves from the temptation to resist, and initiating an action which allows us to move forward is crucial to our growth. It is the shift from being reactive to being proactive. Reaction is clouded by the issues. To paraphrase Einstein, "we cannot find the answers to our problems using the same level of thinking as created them."

We may be initiators, accommodators, or late adapters of change. The further we are down the continuum, the more stagnant our lives will be. Resistance leads to long term, self-inflicted pain.

Choosing to remain stuck, rather than taking the risk of stepping into the unknown, is choosing to suffer needlessly. Geoffrey may survive his personal hell for a while. However, he will be forced to deal with the situation when the heat gets too great. People who use this approach usually lament that they wish they had not waited so long. A personal hell never ends through spontaneous recovery - it only ends when there is a conscious decision to initiate change, followed by an Action Plan.

> *"Life can only be understood backwards, but it must be lived forwards."*
>
> *- Soren Kirkegaard*

Often, change requires a leap of faith. You need to trust your intuition, even if logic and reason hinder you from making the change. Allow your heart to guide you. If you wait until you understand every aspect, and every possible outcome, you will never make any changes.

Time out:

Take a look at your life from the perspective of an outside observer. Where is there resistance to change in your life? Are you an initiator of change, an early adapter, or a late adapter?

Now you See it! Now you Don't!

Sometimes we are deluded. A magician fools us into believing there are bunnies in the hat when there are none. Illusions based on "Now you see it! Now you don't", are based on the idea/belief that if you can't see it - it isn't there. A one year old child learns that mommy doesn't disappear just because he cannot see her anymore. Strangely enough, we continue to be fooled by the magician all our lives.

Our ego is the magician who seeks to confuse us with contradictory messages. It presents an inner dialogue of right and wrong - black and white.

Sometimes people believe everything is right or wrong based on ego - or self-talk. Equally as often, people dismiss their intuition or innate knowledge as an illusion. Self-talk is not spiritual, although sometimes it is mistaken for our spirit.

Self-talk is mortal. The spiritual is not bound by time or space and is immortal. The spiritual is all knowing - a wisdom that surpasses all man-made boundaries and concepts. This aspect of our being is *"in* this world, but not *of* this world" as the Biblical quotation teaches.

Regardless of what we choose to call it, we all have within us a source of inner knowledge. Some people refer to it as the voice of God, or the Creator, or a supreme being. Most people, Christian or non-Christian, have some explanation for this source of wisdom. We cannot reach that source of knowing, unless we silence the voice of the ego, and the external stimuli that compete for our attention. Utilizing this inner knowledge requires meditation, or quiet time alone. The spiritual must not be confused with the voice of our ego that often ties into the fear of change.

Our ego is a busy magician, maintaining an information retrieval system where every stimuli, good or bad, has been stored. He never misplaces a file. He can pull up something from twenty years earlier, faster than the fastest computer, and present it out of context and at the most inconvenient moment. This diligent little magician reminds us frequently that change always means loss.

This magician sends two contradicting messages: a message to resist change (maintaining the status quo), and a message prompted by our internal drive for change and challenge (a drive toward self-actualization). Change then induces, on one side, a fight or flight response. On the other side, a desire to accommodate or initiate change, to resolve the gap between living in mediocrity and living in excellence.

The voice of the magician (our ego), is often interpreted to be the voice of logic and reason. Therefore, it is a key player in our decision making process. Antiquated information can constantly restrain our ability to grow and change. Taking time to clean up the storage system reduces the interference we receive. We need to replace information in the files with new information that will better serve our needs.

Time Out:

Overcoming resistance and fear enables us to become an active initiator of change. Have you reduced the occurrence of involuntary change, and increased your ability to deal effectively with the emotions related to change?

Fortified Failure

Sometimes our reasoning lacks some facts and as a result, may be flawed. Without vital information, we may proceed for a while. We may even seem successful, until our reasoning is put to the test. If it is badly flawed, even the progress we have made may crumble before our very eyes. It is expedient to examine our beliefs for missing pieces of information. Otherwise, we can waste effort on projects which will collapse because they were built without doing our homework first.

The summer when I was twelve, I nominated myself as the construction manager for a tree-fort building project. I considered myself an expert, as my father was a building contractor. His supply of nails, boards, handsaws and ladders was more than adequate for building a dream fort. I decided we should build it spanning three strong branches of three poplar trees. With the 'man' power of six neighbor boys, I commenced to supervise the project. Six weeks later, we had constructed the greatest tree-fort any of us had ever seen.

It was time to put our masterpiece to the test. I climbed up, and jumped on the floor. Then I invited the boys up. I did the count down. When I reached "one" we would all jump in unison on the floor to test its strength. I counted, "three, two, one." There was a terrible crash as everyone fell to the ground! They went home bruised and cut. I went to my bedroom with a bruised ego and lots of scrapes.

The phone began to ring as angry mothers, one after another informed my mother of the disaster. I knew I was in big trouble. Many of the injuries required medical attention. Rather than face the consequences, I decided to dash across the hall to my brother's room, and escape through his window. With my mother on the phone less than five feet from where I needed to cross the hall, this was a big challenge. But, it was the only escape route available. I climbed out the window onto the garage roof, and jumped off the garage.

I rationalized that if I stayed away until well after dark, my parents would be so happy to see me, that they would forgive me. My mother had felt humiliated by the phone calls from the neighbors. When I returned home, she was even more angry than when she first learned about my escapade. My father was proud of my interest in architecture and carpentry, and was quite lenient with me. The conflict between my parents diverted the attention away from me. How often do we divert the attention away from ourselves in an attempt to absolve ourselves of responsibility?

Faulty reasoning, followed by rationalizations, lead to fortified failure. The piece of information I was missing was that you cannot overlap boards and nail them together to make them longer. The missing information may be crucial to our decision making process.

Paradigm Shifts

In the 1950's, a scientist named Thomas Kuhn, developed the concept of the paradigm, as a model of reality. Once we adopt a model of reality, or paradigm, it becomes an operative part of our decisions and actions. We use it to develop and reinforce behaviors that influence every aspect of our lives.

Simply put, paradigms are the belief systems which run our lives. It is not possible to change the way we live our lives, without first changing our belief systems. Any attempt to do so would cause incongruence and a great deal of discomfort.

I am not suggesting that you be contentious. What I am saying is that you must follow your own convictions. You must not sacrifice the right to live your personal truth, just to please

> *"The greatest discovery of my generation is that human beings can alter their lives by altering their attitudes of mind."*
>
> *- William James*

others. Sometimes you need to do things you would rather not do. However, if it requires you to cross ethical and/or moral boundaries, or conflicts with your personal values you need to honor yourself. Let your conscience be your guide.

Sometimes we think one thing and do another. We may do it to conform to the expectations of a teacher, boss, friend or spouse. Deep down inside a voice screams out, "No! No! That isn't the way it is." But we do it anyway. It doesn't feel good, does it? This is incongruence. The same thing happens when we try impression management. Attempting to win the favor of others by pretending, can lead to contradictions between what we believe and what we do.

Have you ever encountered people who change to match their surroundings? They seem to have no personality of their own, and just drift along with everything around them. People who do this lead a very miserable life. Debilitated by low self-esteem, they lose their true identity and drift into apathy. They can stay there and live at zero or they can choose to break free. To break free they must evaluate what they believe and why. The WHY is the really important part. Nature never intended for us to be chameleons.

Becoming locked into faulty paradigms prevents personal growth. It doesn't matter how well the paradigms worked at one time, at some point the paradigm needs to shift. Our environment changes, our personal needs change and the paradigms become ineffective. Continuing to use them stifles growth. Similarly, mimicking others, whether they are family or celebrities, without doing research into why they do things a certain way, is risky business.

Being willing to make regular paradigm shifts enables us to: be open to new information; learn to understand others and our world better; sets us free from mediocrity. Since change happens, whether we plan it or not, the willingness to reformulate our paradigms enables us to control the changes that occur. This is far more effective than just letting change happen as if it is a random experience over which we have no control.

A paradigm shift cannot occur until you begin to question an existing belief. If you fail to

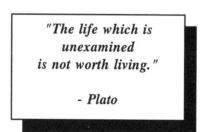

"The life which is unexamined is not worth living."

- Plato

question, you just cruise through life at zero. If you put nothing into life, what would you suppose you would get back out of it? You need to educate yourself, and expose yourself to as much information as you can get. This must be followed by an evaluation stage. This stage is to determine what you are going to do with the information. From all the options, you must determine what you are going to accept and what you are going to discard. The final step is to incorporate the new information into the belief systems which you use to direct your individual life.

Once the change begins, and your vision is clearer, reinforcement becomes the tool that can help you establish new patterns of being. Oral affirmations reinforce reformulated paradigms in your auditory memory. Writing new paradigms out on paper, so they become visual, reinforces our learning through visual learning. Actions based on the new information, store it in the kinesthetic memory. The kinesthetic memory stores the physical or the experiential aspects of a behavioral pattern.

The beliefs you hold, result in habitual ways of dealing with situations. For every negative comment a person receives, he or she needs seven positive comments to balance the effect. Similarly, every time you subconsciously reinforce one of your old paradigms, or old beliefs, in your mind, you need to remind yourself seven times of your new belief.

At first, behavioral change requires conscious thought. As it becomes integrated, the new paradigm will result in unconscious competence. At this point the new behavior is automatic and needs little or no conscious thought. The number of repetitions required before a new pattern is adopted varies greatly. It is influenced by the frequency, the length of time an old habit was practiced, and the amount of distinction between the two models of behavior.

Faulty paradigms, or models of reality, can prevent us from seeing the real potential. It is necessary to be able to identify closed and open belief systems. Some individuals feel threatened when they consider the possibility of examining their paradigms. It is easier for them to adopt the stance of 'what you don't know can't hurt you'. That cliche itself, can be a paradigm which prevents growth.

Our paradigms are shaped by rules made by our parents, society, or religious organizations. Rules are merely codified belief systems, designed to allow for a more harmonious existence between members of a group who accept the governance of the organization. Most often the rules only apply while the group interacts, having little impact on the private lives of the individual group members.

Often, rules come into existence because someone wants control over others. These external sources of control only have power in our lives as long as we accept their control. When we consent to control, we construct our own reality using those rules.

Therefore, it is useful for us to explore the sources of rules we follow in our lives. Are they made by religious organizations, clubs or organizations we belong to, workplace bureaucracies, and/or labor unions and familial hierarchies? Some rules have a valid place in our lives. However, the greater the impact they have on our private lives, the more important it becomes to examine them. Sometimes, even laws are rules made for the convenience of lawmakers.

Breaking a law is illegal, but breaking a law may be a moral action. For instance, it is moral to break the speed limit, if you are doing so to get someone to the hospital in an emergency. But it is still illegal to speed. Most laws have a moral aspect. The whole area of morality versus the law could be debated at length.

Education can enable us to develop new paradigms and open belief systems. Education can allow us to research the sources, challenge the philosophy and more clearly articulate our own intentions and aspirations. This applies to informal learning and formal education.

Developing open belief systems does not imply a lack of values or an "anything goes" attitude. It enables you to see the point of view of other individuals, without feeling any compelling need for consensus. Open-minded people can agree to disagree, without feeling threatened. This also helps individuals understand their own needs and desires more accurately.

Additionally, we need to be able to use creative and critical thinking skills effectively. Both skills are an asset to career decision-making, career search, and within the workplace. They are equally important in the management of our personal lives. Often a person is better at either one or the other of these skills. Using both skills effectively maximizes our ability to initiate and manage transition.

Unfortunately, our school systems, which often rely on conformity to manage classrooms, tend to destroy the natural critical and creative thinking skills of a child. Therefore, adults often lack this skill. Effective creative and critical thinking skills are necessary for solving problems.

Setting goals without analyzing and revising your belief system and values will lead to a future that replicates the past. When your beliefs and values support your intentions and aspirations, you find a source of synergy that propels you toward the future you desire. The ultimate choice is yours, you either live or you exist.

Time out:

Are you holding onto beliefs that serve no useful purpose? How can you develop paradigms which will move you forward? How much would your life change, if you made a regular practice of evaluating your own belief system? Are you exercising your autonomy or are you being controlled by the authority figures and /or institutions which have developed the rules that you follow?

Critical Thinking

Critical thinking is based on analysis. Whether you are analyzing a belief, problem, or situation, the pattern of attack will be approximately the same. Critical thinking is conventional, usually sequential, and could follow these steps:

Step 1   Identify the situation you wish to analyze.

Step 2   Identify the factors that influence the situation or cause the problem.

Step 3   For each cause or factor, create a list of options and/or pros and cons.

Step 4   Gather additional information.

Step 5   Review and evaluate all the alternatives.

Step 6   Evaluate the solutions according to pre-established criteria.

Step 7   Determine which solution is the best.

Step 8   Create an Action Plan based on this choice.

Analytical thinking is objective. Analysis requires detail, accuracy and usually leads to an end that is considered finite and measurable. Creative thinkers, by contrast, find it difficult to imagine that anything has a finite answer, and seldom settle for black and white answers.

A very analytical approach makes it hard to consider the far out, the too simple, or the seemingly impossible solutions. Sometimes, failing to look at the extremes of the situation is the very problem that keeps us stuck in the same rut. There are always more than two choices. An old Chinese proverb teaches, "If there are two solutions, always take the third." Recognizing additional alternatives can be easier if we remove ourselves from the equation, and imagine someone else having to solve the problem. What would someone with a different personality do if they were in your situation?

People who are naturally analytical by nature, are typically found in careers as actuaries, accountants, and scientific research, where meticulous accuracy is mandatory. These are the people who keep a copy of the latest taxation bulletin in their bathroom for leisure reading! They read this kind of stuff, not because they have to, but because - they love it! The thought of changing careers and becoming an actor, or returning to school to study humanities, would seem like an incomprehensible horror. Creativity is difficult for them.

While it is necessary to analyze situations and beliefs, we do not want to be paralyzed by analysis. It is always possible to find a legitimate argument against the very action we need to take. We need to be able to accept the possibility that other choices can be valid, if not for ourselves at least for other people. This is where creative thinking skills can balance the process. Critical thinking, creative thinking, present-centered awareness, releasing the past, and forgiveness, are all assets to our personal growth.

Creative Thinking

Creative thinking gives much more attention to our own intuition. Analytical types are quick to label intuition as irrational thinking. Creative thinking moves beyond the boundaries of the predictable and pays attention to hunches. People who are naturally creative may think of things that would be considered absurd from a logical perspective.

Absurdity is often the catalyst for invention. Creative people often find absolutes difficult to accept. Unlike the accountant types, they see a dozen as twelve or thirteen give or take a little. When told to draw four apples, they add a fifth one just because odd numbers are more aesthetically pleasing.

Intuition may rely on information we hold in our subconscious. We do not need to experience every possible event, to have some opinion about what it would be like. Pairing together some of our experiences, the knowledge acquired from talking with other people, and relating the information to the situation allows us to come to a conclusion.

Therefore, most of our beliefs need to be flexible enough to change over time, and with the addition of new information. For instance, we would not want to still believe the world is flat. Incidentally, why do we draw the shape we draw, when we draw a star? The objects in the universe we call stars, are not actually the shape we draw. This is an example of an old paradigm that has not been revised when new information was available to us.

Creativity requires us to use some subjective thinking. If we are too closely attached to the problem, we are likely to eliminate the options that we feel are too absurd or inappropriate. In doing this we often limit our ability to see new solutions.

Developing creative thinking skills requires practice. Practice by taking one of your beliefs, and listing all the other beliefs that would be possible for the same situation. List, without evaluation, all the possibilities. List all ideas - even the ridiculous, the extreme, and the ones you believe you can without any doubt prove to be wrong.

Write free flowing ideas on Post-it notes and stick them to a mirror. Then, organize the ideas into categories or themes. Generate new ideas from reviewing each theme.

Similarly, writing down an idea and changing it a little at a time can push you to see more creative solutions. Practice making incremental changes to an idea. Each time you add a new idea, fold the paper over, so you will not be distracted by previous ideas. This enables you to recognize there is always a third alternative - as suggested by the Chinese proverb.

When we think there are only two choices, we often dig ourselves out of one pot-hole, just to get stuck in another one. There are many things that can become roadblocks to creativity, and as a result, can stand in our way, when we are seeking to solve a problem. Common barriers to creativity include:

- Fear of change or of challenging the status quo.
- Unwillingness or inability to accept new information.
- Making assumptions without adequate information.
- Lack of ability to take a step back from the situation.
- Procrastination.
- Judgements based on old paradigms.
- Allowing personal perceptions to stand in the way.
- Assuming doing nothing is the easiest or best choice.
- Inclination to be reactive rather than proactive.
- Letting emotions overrule.
- Inability to see the bigger picture.

- Unwillingness to stop and address the situation.
- Assuming time will change the situation.

Decision Making Games

There are many games we can play while we make choices. There are very few beliefs or paradigms that are absolute. Paradigms adopted in one area of a person's life need to fit with other beliefs and values that person holds. One paradigm may be valid for one individual and at the same time would be of no value to another. That is part of the beauty of humanity. We are all individuals. The sooner we can recognize the wisdom in not trying to change others, and in changing only ourselves, the happier we will be.

Most of the games we play are not meaningful. A common decision making game is to do a pros and cons list or a list of advantages and disadvantages. This blocks our own progress. Even when we make a list of many disadvantages, we know that just one advantage can far outweigh all of the disadvantages, or vice versa. If we rationalize all of our choices away, we will end up allowing others to have control over our lives.

Although it may motivate you to change, rebellion is the worst type of motivation. It often has a terrible cost emotionally and physically. Usually it is a reaction to excessive

> *"It is not unusual to find that major changes in life... break the patterns of our lives and reveal to us quite suddenly how much we had been imprisoned by the uncomfortable web we had woven around ourselves. Unlike the jailbird, we don't know that we've been imprisoned until after we've broken out."*
>
> *- John W. Gardner*

control. Examples include: fascism, communism, and sometimes teenagers who have been raised in very controlling homes.

The motivator for change needs to come from within. By nature we have an internal desire to grow and develop. Maslow, the father of self-image psychology, called it self-actualization. Nothing is more painful than remaining in our stuck condition. Nothing can provide us with more freedom than taking control of our own destiny.

Time out:

What are some of the decision making games that you play? What are some more effective problem solving strategies which you could use?

Chapter 4

Beyond Belief

> *"In the middle of the journey of our life I came to myself within a dark wood where the straight way was lost. Ah, how hard a thing it is to tell of that wood, savage and harsh and dense, the thought of which renews my fear.*
> *So bitter is it that death is hardly more."*
>
> *- Dante Alighhiere at age 37*
> *(opening of Divine Comedy)*

Lemonade or Champagne

Lemons are great if you are looking for pucker power. People who appear to suck lemons every morning before coming to work, aren't going to be noticed for their pucker power. Sour people repel rather than attract other people. Lemonade may be a great refresher on a hot afternoon, but it is hardly something you want to use as a staple in your diet.

There may be times when you need to follow the advice of the quotation "If life hands you lemons - make lemonade." However, is lemonade all you want out of life? If you are planting lemon trees, watering lemon trees, fertilizing lemon trees and harvesting lemons, you can hardly expect anything more than lemonade as an end product. Most of us remember our childhood lemonade stands. They didn't become Fortune 500 companies, did they?

Yet, we frequently adopt cliches like this and create the reality they describe, without so much as thinking about the process. Then we feel bitter disappointment. If we intend to end up with champagne instead of lemonade, we need to cultivate grapes, not lemon trees. Do the slogans which you have adopted support your intentions?

The 'lemonade' cliche was intended, in all likelihood, to promote the value of endurance and tenacity. These are good qualities, but there are situations which should not be endured. An intolerable job, or an abusive relationship are things that should not be endured. The tenacity of an individual who continues to choose to stay in these situations, is scarcely admirable.

Our beliefs are the most powerful determinants of our future. Unless we are willing to move *beyond the beliefs* which hold us prisoners, we will never reach our true potential. Recognizing and changing irrational beliefs can result in transition that will be, *beyond belief* for most of those who observe. They simply will not understand how it is possible to succeed in making such dramatic transformation.

Sometimes we buy into the philosophies of others as if we were buying sale items at a wholesale buyer's club. We use rationalizations like "Everyone else is doing it." Buying into other people's philosophies may not be a good deal, unless we want the results that come along with the philosophies. The purchase may be a good decision - if we want or need the product. Buying three cases of 24 heads of lettuce is not a bargain; unless you operate a restaurant or a catering company where you can utilize them. We can do the same thing with slogans or cliches. They may not apply in the context where we use them. The slogan may be an excuse, used to avoid having to deal with the real question.

However, criticizing or passing judgement on a person who fails to exercise choices, is not an asset to anyone. One person has no right to judge the decisions or actions of another person. Awareness always precedes the recognition of the presence of choices. When an individual chooses to live in a limited or self-restricted reality, he or she has access to a limited number of options.

It is possible to be so stuck that one cannot see any alternative. Often, an abused spouse is so traumatized by the circumstances that the ability to reason and understand alternatives is totally swept aside in the struggle to survive.

Yet, to exist under those conditions takes a tremendous amount of tenacity and personal power. The problem is that the effort is misdirected. The more difficult the situation, the more indication there is that the person has tremendous inner strength.

When this inner strength is refocussed in the right direction, the survivors of abuse are capable of unprecedented growth. The change occurs when they recognize the choices and choose to set themselves free. As they begin to utilize the resources and remove the barriers to change, they become dynamic and marvelous people who are not just surviving - but thriving.

Choosing to make lemonade after you have toured the winery and experienced the bubbly, is choosing to stay stuck. Some survivors choose to suck lemons for years, even when trauma no longer exists. Survivors who seize the opportunity to grow and thrive become filled with the *bubbles of joy* that come from living with excellence.

Time out:

Are you making lemonade? How many bubbles are there in your champagne? Have you bought into philosophies that are ineffective? Who is the wholesaler of philosophies in your life?

The Joy of Suffering

When we really understand our true potential, we move from needing to be motivated, to a state of passion. Motivation, by dictionary definition, is the act or process of furnishing with an incentive or inducement into action. *Inducement* or *incentive* suggest an external source of control. That is why motivation is temporary, and rarely works very well.

Paying five hundred dollars for a fitness membership may induce temporary incentive but it won't provide passion. Guilt is experienced when the motivation wears off, and you quit going.

Passion is the ingredient that keeps the professional athlete in the game after: the pinned femur, knee surgery, four concussions, three broken noses, and a broken jaw. It is why the athlete becomes a coach, when age dictates the end of a career as a player.

Passion comes from the root word *passio* which means "to suffer for." When we are filled with passion, we have an impelling internal force that is so strong, it becomes harder for us to remain in a state of inaction, than it is for us to act. It is like desire fuelled by adrenalin.

It must come from within, as that is where the source of our innate potential to thrive resides. The silence of meditation and suspending conflicting influences of the ego are crucial steps in accessing our spiritual self. The ability to communicate with our life spirit frees us to passionately reach toward our unlimited potential.

Time out:

Last time you acted on your motivation how long did it last? What is motivating you? Can others feel your passion? What is your passion?

Uneven Playing Fields

Joe believed the government was wasting taxpayers' dollars on life prolonging procedures...until his son needed a liver transplant. Jacqui thought drunk drivers should have their licences suspended...until it was she who was caught.

> *"Principles are to people what roots are to trees. Without roots, trees fall when they are thrashed with the winds of a storm. Without principles, people fall when they are shaken by the gales of life."*
>
> *- Carlos Reyles*

Connie borrowed her boss' company car and returned it later than she promised...something unexpected came up and she couldn't get back in time, so she kept the car overnight. But, when Connie's boss was late getting her paycheque signed, Connie reported him to the Employee Standards Branch.

Melinda won't take the extra office chair home...that's dishonest. She has phoned in sick however, and collected sick-pay for nine days in the past year. Three of the sick days were used to go to Las Vegas. Six days were used to go shopping.

It may seem unlikely that a person would have contradictory beliefs in operation at the same time, however it is very common. Inconsistencies are frequently wrapped around tentative wording: "I think I probably could," "Sometime I might," "I should try it," and similar phrases. Or in language that absolves us of carrying through: "I think that...but...", "usually, except when...", or similar language. Words like "but" or "except" cancel the meaning of the first part of the sentence. We contradict ourselves when we say we believe one thing and do another. It may be an attempt to conceal our fear of how others will respond.

What we do in one area of our life affects all the other areas. It is not possible to operate by different rules, in different aspects of our lives, without running into conflict with our own beliefs. It leads to inner turmoil, because we are ignoring values we believe to be important. This leads to remorse or guilt, which are often followed by rationalizations. We may rationalize that uncomfortable feelings are based on the unwillingness of others to give us a "break."

> *"I know of no safe depository of the ultimate powers of society but the people themselves; and if we think them not enlightened enough to exercise their control with a wholesome discretion, the remedy is not to take it from them, but to inform their discretion by education."*
>
> *- Thomas Jefferson*

Contradictions are often found in relationships with other people. Others view people with contradictory beliefs as untrustworthy and they believe they do not care about the feelings of anyone except themselves. We need to be open to new information and flexible enough to understand the views of others, but our beliefs cannot be amorphous.

> *"What lies behind us and what lies before us are tiny matters compared to what lies within us."*
>
> *- William Morrow*

Analyzing our own beliefs for discrepancies like this can assist us in gaining inner peace. We need to take a serious look at the beliefs we operate by, and how we developed them before we can move on. Some of our beliefs may be very healthy, and others may require revision. Revision stems from the word vision. A clear vision is the foundation for passion and excellence.

Once we have evaluated our beliefs, and have decided on our own values, we can articulate our vision. Clearly defined beliefs and values support one another, enabling us to achieve our aspirations and intentions with far less effort. Rather than it being difficult to attain our goals, we become actively involved in the flow of creation - creating a future that will be fulfilling and meaningful.

Incongruence causes a cacophony of emotions. Congruence in all areas of our life creates internal harmony. Taking action, which is consistent with our internal principles, creates a peaceful melody that is in tune with our internal well-being and external environment.

Time out:

Have you evaluated your beliefs and revised them to support your growth? Do you have beliefs in one area of your life that conflict with the beliefs in other areas? Do you have one set of rules for yourself and another for other people?

Getting Unstuck

We weren't stuck...or were we? The big semi-trailers jack-knifed in the ditch...they were stuck. The cars in the ditch, they were stuck. But us...no - we were still on the road. We couldn't move anymore...but that was beside the point. The reason we couldn't move was because the mud was stuck to us, not that we were stuck in the mud...one of my earliest childhood recollections provides an excellent metaphor for understanding how we often react when we are emotionally stuck in life.

I was only four that summer. My parents and my uncle decided to take a trip to a small community only a few miles from the border of the Northwest Territories. Their motivation for going was strong, and they intended to let nothing prevent them from reaching their destination.

The mud clinging to our tires had completely filled the wheel wells. The tires could no longer turn. Dad got out and took the shovel from the trunk. When he reached the trunk, his boots were so caked with mud that he had to shovel them off before he could walk back to the tires.

Roads in those days were not like the roads of today. It had been raining heavily for days. The soil in the area is rich in silt and becomes very sticky when it gets wet. To imagine the consistency of this particular type of mud, known as gumbo, think of it as mud which is attracted to itself and to everything else.

The number of cars in the ditches seemed to exceed the number of cars on the road, on this lonely stretch of highway. My father and

> *"This life, therefore, is not righteousness but growth in righteousness, not health but healing, not being but becoming, not rest but exercise. We are not yet what we shall be, but we are growing toward it. The process it not yet finished, but it is going on. This is not the end, but it is the road."*
>
> *- Martin Luther*

uncle took turns driving, as we inched our way along, taking care not to become the next car in the ditch. This was a real life survival course.

Even as we drove, the mud accumulated around the tires until it was impossible for the tires to turn. Either dad or my uncle would take their turn at shovelling the mud off the tires and out of the wheel wells, so we could proceed again.

I am not sure if it was my fear of getting stranded, or the humor of the amount of mud that accumulated on their boots, which imbedded this experience on my memory. Before they could get back in the car, they would have to clean the mud off their feet, using first the shovel and then a stick. A distance that should have taken four hours lasted two days.

Getting stuck and getting moving again is, in itself, a difficult experience. Getting stuck repeatedly is devastating. Some people sadly lose the focus of their destination, then rationalize that the destination wasn't that important, and just give up. They suppress the truth. Some people who do this become overwhelmed with fear and disappointment. Eventually they are filled with apathy, or they erupt in uncontrolled insecurities, cynicism and bitterness.

For some individuals, the pain is turned inward, causing depression. For others, the pain is exhibited outwardly, in the form of aggression. Generally speaking, depression and passivity are more common in women; while anger and aggression are more often exhibited by men. Present-centered awareness is replaced with detachment. This is avoiding reality. When we do not want to deal with the present, we first build fences, then walls. The building blocks for these walls are false beliefs and rationalizations.

Before these barriers can be removed, it is necessary to recognize they exist. We must first recognize that we are stuck. Then we must find and use tools to remove the mud that hinders us. We must dismantle the walls and fences, and set ourselves free to move forward to our unlimited potential. Faulty beliefs and conditioned behaviors cause us to ignore our innate ability to live self-directed lives.

> *"Only that day dawns to which we are awake."*
>
> *-Henry David Thoreau*

As you set yourself free to enjoy the journey of life, you will soon recognize things from the past that you no longer wish to retain. You will be burning bridges on the roads you no longer want to travel, and you will enjoy the journey. As new horizons move into your vision, you will proceed with confidence, enjoying the course you design for yourself, adding further destinations as your vision clears.

Time out:

Have you allowed yourself time for self-discovery? Have you acknowledged the gap between your present reality and your ideal reality? Have you released the past? What are some of the resources you recognize and utilize? Can you identify gain and loss in the changes you are making in your life? What faulty beliefs are barriers to your personal change?

Section II

Wholeness
Is the Sum of the Parts

"This above all:
to your own self be true,
and it must follow as
the night the day,
you cannot then
be false to any person. "

- William Shakespeare

Chapter 5

A Spiritual Quest

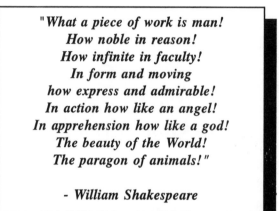

"What a piece of work is man!
How noble in reason!
How infinite in faculty!
In form and moving
how express and admirable!
In action how like an angel!
In apprehension how like a god!
The beauty of the World!
The paragon of animals!"

- William Shakespeare

From the Inside Out

Self-image is often linked to things, possessions, jobs, other people and our homes. This self-image is ego based. The true self is a spiritual being which transcends the boundaries of time and space. Our spiritual-self is boundless, eternal and infinite.

Our lives here are only the physical manifestation of a much larger concept of self. We have no true need to achieve anything beyond our own intentions and aspirations. We trap ourselves on an endless treadmill as long as we measure who we are by the tangibles around us. Attempting to accommodate the desires of others can hinder our growth. If we place too much importance on the opinions of others, we may deny our true identity.

Understanding the magnitude of our existence, as something that is not limited to our earthly experience, enables us to transcend our ego state. When we understand our inner strength, the realm of possibilities for our lives becomes infinite. We understand why our choices are the only things that limit us. We become individuated - knowing that we are complete in ourselves but that we can choose to be mutually interdependent with others.

When we have become self-actualized individuals, we then are ready to develop healthy relationships with other people. We are no longer willing to participate in co-dependent relationships, and we have much more to contribute. We have learned to give without depleting our own resources. Through giving we generate more energy for ourselves.

Within our true self there is an individual inner truth. It is part of human existence. When we respond to our inner truth, we are willing to lay aside differences based on culture, ethnic background, and heritage. To understand others, we must open channels for discussion on as many fronts as possible. The spiritual-self values others, honors human dignity, is without malice, is charitable, caring and honest. Awareness of the spiritual prompts us to ask for help, and to think with the heart as well as with the head. It is being aware of the bigger picture as events unfold. It is being able to harmonize the advice we receive from the outside, with the internal guidance of our inner truth.

The Quest of Spiritual Beings

Life is a spiritual quest. The human body is the

> *"Each path is only one of a million paths. Therefore, you must always keep in mind that a path is only a path. If you feel that you must now follow it, you need not stay with it under any circumstances. Any path is only a path. There is no affront to yourself or others in dropping it if that is what your heart tells you to do."*
>
> *-Carlos Castenada*

embodiment of our spirit. The evolution of society, in many ways, has trivialized this aspect of our existence. We have placed more value on rules, norms and standards set by various levels of society.

Individually, we must find our truth and live it. The solutions for one person may not be appropriate for another. Often we fail to find the right answer because we limit ourselves to two choices. For instance, a woman takes her car to the mechanic because it is not working well, and she cannot afford a better car. The mechanic informs her that the car needs repairs which will cost $2400. This verdict may make her frustrated and defensive if she believes the mechanic is solving his own financial problems at her expense. It may seem like the only choices are to spend the money or stop driving the car.

The woman can either be distracted by her emotions, or she can search out a more effective solution. Her options may include: getting a second opinion, using recycled parts, finding a source of additional income, or re-evaluating her personal spending habits. Accepting the mechanic's reality is not necessarily going to provide serenity or harmony for her. The answers are always available, but often they are not obvious.

The spirit within can guide us to thrive. The more connected we are to our spirituality, the greater our level of awareness will be. Present centered awareness, means separating oneself from the fetters of the past and setting oneself free from future enchantment.

Absolving oneself of the responsibility for making changes today, wastes the opportunity to create a meaningful future. Any idyllic future we imagine, but do not actively participate in, is just an illusion. Constantly fantasizing leads to a schizophrenic view of the world.

The schizophrenic is separated from reality, and lives in an illusion. Living in this state, imagining reality to be the illusion and imagining illusions to be reality, is the most paralyzed state of mind we can experience. The resulting paranoia leads to an inability to act. In this existence there is no peace, no fulfilment, no joy, and no passion - only endless emotional pain.

Focussing on the present frees us to celebrate our spiritual self. Our spiritual being is gentle, like an angel. It retreats when the conditions are not conducive to its gentle nature. Our life spirit makes itself manifest in times of stillness and quietness. Allowing ourselves time to meditate, or to be quiet and alone, is of great value in honoring our spirituality.

When we allow the energies of harmony, joy and love to prevail, nature's intelligence can function with effortless ease. When we are spiritually in tune, we have less desire to convince others of our viewpoint. We are more willing to accept others and the universe as a whole. We stop struggling with our environment and become present centered creators of our ideal reality.

When we attempt to create our future based only on logic, we close our access to the intuitive. Our intuition does not judge; it is not convoluted by the concepts of winners and losers. Our life spirit connects to every source of energy within us, and every source of energy outside of us. It can guide us to the most effortless way of creating a future which corresponds to our intentions and aspirations.

Intuition is the lubricant which reduces the friction between *what is* and the realm of unlimited possibilities. Visualizing a reality without boundaries and accepting responsibility for our choices frees us to enjoy life to the fullest.

Future Vision

> *"Every man has the right to feel that 'because of me was the world created.' "*
>
> *-Talmud*

We call certain people, visionaries. They seem to be able to see things before other people do, and are innovators of new ideas. These people are no more intelligent than you or I, and they do not have access to any power that we cannot also access. Clearing our vision requires temporary suspension of logic and judgement, which are restraints to creativity.

When we see possibilities and then use rationalizations to think of all the reasons why they cannot occur, we cloud our vision. Our clearest vision comes from allowing the negative aspects of our past experience to be swept away. This allows the illusions of *what could be* in the future to be replaced with present centered awareness.

The power for busting loose comes from within. In this respect, the process of human transition is congruent with the process of change demonstrated in nature around us. The force that brings about new life comes from within.

When it is given the right conditions for growth every source of new life in nature evolves in a series of transitions. The living organism is programmed with all the information necessary for growth. We must remove the barriers that prevent our growth. Once our passion is set free it enables us to grow and develop. The passion is charged with an energy force that fuels the process of change. The process of personal change is comparable to the metamorphosis in the development of the butterfly.

Metamorphosis

**Think
of the power
from within, that
enables the butterfly
to emerge from the cocoon.
A butterfly is so delicate and fragile
-and still without damaging that fragility,
the butterfly emerges from the cocoon
to spread its beautiful wings and
fill its purpose in the ecology.
Imagine if the pupa allowed
FEAR to keep it
... in the cocoon.**

Our *comfort zone* is our cocoon. Fear or procrastination can increase the length of time spent in a pupa-like state, as an undeveloped human. When you develop wings so you can fly, you become a beautiful human being. A person so warm, loving, in tune with self and others - that people covet the same for themselves.

Empowered individuals are cognizant of a spiritual connection and honor all humanity. Their intentions and desires are motivated by a value system that neither harms others nor the environment. Spiritual awareness impels them to live by the golden rule.

If we have a vision and no plan to make that vision a reality then it is only an illusion. Powerful people are able to make their vision a reality. Power is the ability to do and act. Those who are most successful spend little time thinking about how difficult their experiences have been, and only see them as opportunities for growth.

A Diamond in the Rough

Many times difficult experiences are the result of wrong choices. There is no wisdom in chiding ourselves, or others, for past choices that have led to difficult experiences. However, if we understand our choices and decide to remain unchanged, our suffering becomes voluntary.

Clench your fist as tight as possible and hold it for two or three minutes. Then try to straighten out your fingers. Then try to pick up a small object. Your fingers will feel almost numb, and it affects your ability to pick up the object. This is what happens when you hang on to mistakes or hurts from the past. You become partially paralyzed and unable to act. Without action there can be no progress.

Many individuals create a personal hell for themselves and then remain there, because they are paralyzed with fear. We have conditioned ourselves to prefer the known to the unknown. Fear is the product of an imaginary reality that we have chosen to construct based on an imagined outcome. Change, even for the better, involves temporary loss.

One of the most unforgettable characters from my childhood, was an old man named Frank, who frequently invited our family for Sunday dinner. In my childish way of thinking, he seemed to be the ugliest man I had ever seen, but he had a beauty which was very deep. His face was disfigured from shrapnel injuries. He had one glass eye, an artificial leg, and limited mobility in his right arm. His war injuries left him in a condition that could have caused him to give up, but he didn't. And that was not all.

He had lost his home three times to fire. The first fire was a chimney fire, the second was caused by a kerosene lamp, and the third was caused by lightning. In the second fire he lost his infant son. In the third fire he lost his loving wife and his two young daughters. Although he managed to get them out of the house, they died of smoke inhalation. His arms and face were scarred from burns he received in his attempt to save his family.

He was poverty stricken, but he refused to be lonely or to feel sorry for himself. On his little acreage, he grew a big garden, and kept a few pigs and chickens. He entertained twelve to eighteen dinner guests every Sunday. Wooden apple and orange crates served as chairs. The table was a sheet of plywood suspended on two wooden saw horses. An old white bedsheet was used as a tablecloth. None of the dishes matched. His three room house was so small that there was no room to walk around the "table," once it was set up.

On the embankment along the road, he planted and tended a host of beautiful flowers. Irises, lilies, peonies, daisies, marigolds, portulaca, chrysanthemums and other flowers were enjoyed by people from miles away.

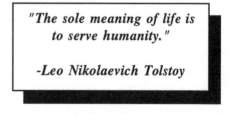

"The sole meaning of life is to serve humanity."

-Leo Nikolaevich Tolstoy

White birch trees stood in contrast to the well-manicured lawn. In this area there were seldom ninety frost-free days in a year, making this prize winning garden even more of a feat.

People made special trips to show their visitors his garden. They got out of their cars and took pictures. Most of them didn't even know who lived there, much less the story behind the man.

Frank was known by many children, because he carried peppermints in his pocket. They would run to meet him. He never talked much, but the children would skip along beside him, as he whistled a monotone tune. He had found a way to partially fill the void created by the family he had lost.

He never complained, and frequently admonished others for complaining. Frank was a contributor, and most of the recipients of his efforts did not know the past hardships he had experienced. I did not know the story of the fires, or the reason for his disfiguring scars, until after his death.

Ten years after Frank died, I drove by that property. The setting that was once like a botanical garden, was overgrown with weeds. The yard was cluttered with retired cars, tattered sofas, old tires and the like. It was the same piece of property with the same potential. The present owners lacked the vision and the willingness to take action to recreate the beautiful garden.

Often, the definitions we create for disabilities are so inappropriate. Rather than labelling disabilities, we need to recognize that we all have different challenges and abilities. More often than not, the biggest difference is in our perception of the situation, and not in the actual circumstance.

The biggest barriers are emotional barriers we create for ourselves. Ray Charles, Stevie Wonder, and John Milton, (author of Paradise Lost) though physically blind, were not blind to possibility. Helen Keller was blind and could not hear or speak. As a child Walt Disney was told he had no talent. Bill Wilson a "hopeless" alcoholic, founded Alcoholics Anonymous. Louis Pasteur was rated mediocre in chemistry. Grandma Moses was eighty when she started painting. These people overcame barriers and lived fulfilling lives.

You too can make a difference. If your personal experiences have been hard, just think of diamonds. They are made of carbon, which under different circumstances is a soft substance.

Extraordinary!

**Carbon is found everywhere,
cojoined with its favorite friends hydrogen and oxygen.
Plants and animals are formed by these elements
when joined together as one.
But carbon alone
under extreme heat and pressure
forms a hard and beautiful substance.
A rare substance called the diamond.
"It takes one thousand tonnes of pressure
per square inch and a million degrees" scientists say.
So beautiful, and strong.
Chosen to symbolize everlasting love.
Some people are like the treasured diamond.
Their strength comes from
heat and burdens hard to bear.
They speak not of the pain.
Their strength of character and inner
beauty they with others share.**

Time out:
Are you allowing self-manufactured disabilities to hinder your
potential? Does your vision match your full potential? Are you taking
action to make the vision become a reality?

Harmony from Within

It is not possible to have synchromeshed beliefs and values if we have adopted our beliefs and values from other people, or from social groups. We cannot take ownership of beliefs unless we analyze them to determine if they are compatible with our personal philosophy. Attempting to honor incongruent concepts leads to confusion.

Belief analysis is hard work. However, unless we take the time to do it, we will not be building our lives on a strong foundation. Imagine printing a measuring tape on wide sewing elastic. If we use a measuring tool that is not dependable, the results will be different every time. This leads to powerless behavior. It leads to going around and around in circles.

Our values need not stay the same forever, however we need to be clear about why we change them, if we do. They are the guideposts for our actions and goal posts for our progress.

Our Vision Statement needs to be based on a set of values that we are not willing to compromise. This enables us to live in a state of harmony, and makes it easier to be in tune with our spiritual self.

Clear Intentions

Clear intentions and a written Vision Statement, make it much easier for us to know where we are going. If you hardly know what you expect of yourself, it is not possible for others to know what to expect of you either. Clarity contributes to trust, cooperation from others, and team spirit.

Being clear in your intentions starts at a personal level. You need to be honest with yourself. It enables you to be consistent in your actions. This results in less susceptibility to distractions and more stability. Checking our visual acuity regularly can enable us to stay on track and assist us in reaching our goals.

The Dead Man's Money

Knowing he had little time left, a miserly man asked an accountant, a lawyer and a politician, to his bedside. He told each one that he had $15,000 hidden in his home. He asked each one to put the money in an

"Hateful to me as the gates of hell is he, who hiding one thing in his heart, utters another."

-Homer
The Illiad

envelope and just as his casket was being closed, to throw the envelope in.

The accountant would find the money under the mattress and the lawyer would find the money in a sock in the bottom drawer. The politician was to find the money in the coffee can in the cupboard. Each one assumed the man had only the $15,000, because they were unaware of the requests asked of the other two. At the funeral, each completed her task, but they were overcome with curiosity and decided to discuss their assignments.

The accountant explained that the man had told her where she would find $15,000. She prepared an audited statement, then decided to exchange the small bills for larger bills at the bank so it wouldn't be so bulky to carry. This meant she had to provide a second audited statement. She had calculated the fees for services rendered, and deducted that from the total. She accordingly placed the statements and the remaining $7,354.78 in the envelope.

The lawyer confessed that she too had been instructed to find $15,000. She said she was surprised at the accountant's gullibility. She said "Having found the money, I advertised that I had found an undisclosed amount of money and that if anyone could provide the serial numbers, they could claim it." She further stated, "the verdict isn't in yet, so I deposited the money in a trust account and provided the man with a cheque as security in case he somehow could still lay claim to the money."

The politician stated that the man had told her she too would find $15,000. Although she had found the money, the self-serving politician decided to deny it. "The old man must have been confused," she stated, "because all I found was a statement of income tax arrears. However, I also noticed he had some valuable antiques," she continued. "I have made arrangements for the tax department to seize them in order to clear his tax arrears," concluded the politician.

The true test of our integrity is not what we do when others are watching - it is what we do when we know absolutely for sure that others can't find out. Integrity is a state of being whole and complete. It is the quality built by keeping our commitments to other people.

Integrity is the demonstrated strength to complete the task, even when it gets difficult. Sometimes, that means you need to face circumstances you would rather avoid, and it may call for tenacity. Broken promises destroy integrity. Honoring your word may mean a personal sacrifice.

Integrity is lost when competitiveness replaces harmony. It is not dependent on profit, or mood, or the time of day or the duration of the commitment. Integrity is founded on honesty and is not hard for others to recognize.

The politician was dishonest with others, and was also dishonest with herself. When I was in grade nine, my mother decided the novel assigned by my teacher was inappropriate reading material. Rather than tell the teacher, which was intensely embarrassing to me, I tried to fake it. I read the dust jacket and the first and last chapter. I was naive enough to think that Mrs. Fleming, my teacher, had not read the book.

My lack of honesty got me into deeper problems when Mrs. Fleming decided to punish me by making me write three book reports. When we are not whole and complete, we hurt ourselves more than we hurt others. Feigned integrity often crumbles at the first test.

Time out:
What would you have done with the dead man's money? Have you broken commitments which need to be repaired before you can move forward?

Unconditional Love

Our life spirit is based on unconditional love. Our spiritual side is unfamiliar with hate, contempt and discord. There is no surer way of becoming disconnected from our spiritual guide, than by allowing any of these three traits or emotions to have a place in our lives.

Learning to love yourself is the most powerful thing you can do to increase your growth potential. In our culture, we often speak of love and peace, while demonstrating the opposite. Lack of peace destroys trust. Without trust, love cannot survive.

Whether conflict is internal or external, personal or societal, the answer does not utilize tactics and tools that caused the problem in the first place. When we tap into our spiritual source of power, we find answers that are more meaningful than the answers coming from logic and reason.

Unconditional love is born of the spiritual, manifests no malice, and endures the test of time. Unconditional love for all humanity surpasses racial differences or the differences in economic status. It extends beyond the boundaries of our earth-bound experiences.

Chapter 6

Emotional Energies

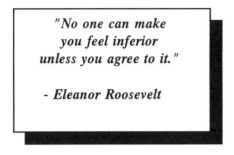

> *"No one can make*
> *you feel inferior*
> *unless you agree to it."*
>
> *- Eleanor Roosevelt*

Emotions

We are emotional beings. There are six basic emotions: love, joy, surprise, anger, fear and sadness. These are fairly easy for us to understand. More complex emotions are mixtures of these six and are more difficult for us to understand. Our emotions interact with the emotions of others. Sometimes they are in harmony, and sometimes they are not. Even when we attempt to understand our feelings and express them to others, misunderstandings occur.

When their eyes interlocked in class, Debbie knew this was the one. This was love at first sight. The feelings were mutual. Jim promptly asked her out.

He borrowed his older brother's '57 Chevy, and took Debbie to the drive-in. They did what all the other teenagers who go to the drive-in movies do...they watched the movie. After twenty minutes of movie watching, Jim asked Debbie if she wanted to get into the back seat.

Debbie declined. So they did more movie watching...and twenty minutes later, he asked again. Debbie declined. She, after all, was very clear about her emotions. Jim persisted, and asked for the fourth time, "would you like to get in the back seat now?"

Debbie responded without hesitation "No, thank-you, I prefer to stay here in the front with *YOU!*"

Their emotions were a by-product of their desires and beliefs. Jim hoped that he could change Debbie's desires. When he was unsuccessful, his beliefs about himself, her, and the situation altered his emotions.

Jim never asked her out again. So what's new? The problem is still the same - when one gender expresses emotions, the other gender just doesn't get it! Although it seems quite simple, emotions are often very complex.

We are not always aware of our mental state. Debbie and Jim appraised the same situation, but each experienced feelings that were complex and unique to the individual. Most of the time the appraisal occurs on the subconscious level. If we think about our emotions, we become more aware of them and can control them to a great extent. However, in some ways, thinking about our feelings, can complicate the process of controlling them. Thinking about them may evoke another emotion, making it more difficult for us to sort out our feelings.

Emotion is generated by the appraisals we make of the changes we experience, in Debbie's case by the close encounter. If Debbie avoided the date, it would have resulted in less emotion. Perhaps even a greater danger is that we would think about our emotions and decide we should ignore or deny them. Avoiding change or suppressing emotions leads to stagnation and a state of emotional numbness.

Conversely, a state of emotional awareness supports personal growth. Happiness, for example, results when we perceive a change as positive. For us to remain happy, then, we need to continue to make those changes which we are going to perceive as enjoyable. (No, that doesn't mean Jim needed a new date every night!) Conditions that correspond to our desires and our perception of self-fulfilment induce happiness. We have more opportunities to feel fulfilled if we broaden our interests.

Emotions are relative, and are greatly influenced by what we use as a comparison. A man who breaks his leg may be happy, because he compares himself to another person who is permanently confined to a wheel chair. Whereas another man who earns $100,000 a year may be unhappy because he compares his financial situation to that of the richest person in America.

Each of us holds erroneous beliefs that are not conducive to our mental well-being. It is unrealistic to expect ourselves to respond differently, unless we first revise the beliefs that affect our appraisals, and the comparisons we use.

Our innate tendency is to strive for constant personal development, or self-actualization. Although outside influences alter our feelings, a positive mental attitude makes a great difference. Creating an emotionally sound environment for ourselves promotes growth and development.

Time out:

What are your interests? Time yourself and see how many interests you can list in two minutes. Which ran out first, your list of interests or the two minutes? Are you generally happy? What do you measure your emotions against - your past experiences or the imagined fantasy of someone else's reality?

Expressing Mixed Emotions

The salesman was feeling ambivalent as he approached the door. He felt anxious about last night's date...frustrated with his boss...curious about the anonymous phone call he had received...perplexed by the previous customer's response, and jealous of his brother's success. Little did he know that behind the door there was a woman who was disappointed by her sister...enraged by the clogged drain...bored with the laundry...exasperated by her son's mess...hurt by her best friend...disgusted at the cost of living, and lonely because it doesn't seem anyone understands. Whose emotions have the most to do with the door being slammed in the salesman's face?

Our ability to be understood by others is greatly dependent on our ability to understand ourselves. Increasing the number of words we use to describe our emotions, enhances our ability to deal with them. In a workshop environment, I ask participants to list as many emotions as they can think of...some get stuck after the first six or eight words. There are at least seventy-five words in the English language that describe emotions. Increasing your vocabulary by an additional twenty words is a powerful way to increase self-understanding, and subsequently, others' understanding of you.

Often, our feelings are expressed by our body language, even when we do not express them in any other way. The body language demonstrating anger, fear, sadness, joy, surprise and love seems to be uniform across all cultures. The experiences that trigger each emotion may vary from culture to culture. An aboriginal person from the jungle may respond in fear if taken for a ride in a glass elevator. A North American may feel fear if he or she encounters certain jungle animals. Each individual would see the other person's apprehension as unfounded.

> *"I've hundreds of things to say, but my tongue just can't manage them. So I'll dance them for you."*
>
> *- Nikos Kazantzakis*
> *Zorba the Greek*

Fear creates a barrier to change. Often it is irrational. My fear of bridges started when I was four. In spring, the river valley between my parent's and my grandparent's homes flooded. My father would check the depth of the water and see that the bridge had not washed out. I was too terrified to cross in the car. My dad had to carry me to the other side and leave me there until he drove across. Without a doubt I would have been safer in the car than I was standing on the road. There would have been adequate time for me to wander into the water, slip and drown. Seeing as I was fond of wading in mud puddles, this was a far higher risk than for me to be in the car.

As I grew older, I missed many adventures because I lacked the courage to cross certain bridges. Dad loved to explore, and often we encountered condemned bridges. If it was at all possible, he would cross and follow the trail to its end. When I was not willing to take the risk, I missed the adventures on the other side.

When I was about eleven, we visited a pedestrian suspension bridge that crossed a wide river. It was extremely unstable and had ten-foot wire fencing to protect the pedestrians from falling into the river. Large warning signs explained the danger, and listed young children and seniors as people who should stay off the bridge. In big letters it said DANGER! CROSS AT YOUR OWN RISK. It was a very windy day, which made crossing the bridge even more difficult and dangerous.

We could see the rugged badlands, hoodoos, and old mines on the other side. I wanted to go exploring and knew that I would miss out on a lot of fun if I didn't go along. That day, I confronted my long standing fear of bridges.

The danger was very real - later that summer the bridge was permanently closed. My father stated it was the most dangerous bridge he had ever crossed. However, our success in crossing that bridge made all my fear of bridges seem trivial. Courage is action taken realizing the risks are challenges, not barriers. Today, rural bridges hold special meaning to me. They are symbolic of a transition and going beyond the known to discover the unknown.

More complex feelings are evoked in response to specific situations, and are influenced by values, beliefs, cultural and social conditioning. Our response can be altered by examining and changing the underlying beliefs and values.

Attitudes and emotions interact very closely. Attitudes are based on how we feel and our beliefs about a subject or object. Being mentally healthy and having a good attitude is dependent on our paradigms. Therefore, nothing will change unless we change our paradigms.

Mental well-being depends greatly on the ability to deal effectively with one's emotions. Failure to deal with negative emotions before they escalate, can result in emotional outbursts. Suppressed emotions do not go away: they come back later. Then it is often unclear as to what is causing them. Dealing with them in the present makes it easier to attribute the emotions to the right causes. Our ability to deal with our emotions effectively, builds our self-image or self-esteem.

Time out:
How many words that describe emotions can you list in two minutes? Do you suppress your feelings? Does fear prevent you from moving forward? Do you have the courage to overcome the barriers?

Self-Esteem

When she was seven, my daughter wrote, "when I grow up I am gonna be like mom, and teach people to get some of that self-a-steam-stuff." Although she didn't spell it right, she had

> *"It is thus with most of us; we are what other people say we are. We know ourselves chiefly by hearsay."*
>
> *- Eric Hoffer*

a better understanding of self-esteem at seven, than many of us do when we are adults. I, like many of my peers, reached adulthood without any understanding of self-esteem. In addition to not knowing what it was, I didn't have even a shred of it.

Self-esteem is often based on the appraisals of others. This can lead to a vicious circle that interferes with our personal development. The cycle many of us get trapped in is as follows:

- We act.
- Others react.
- We interpret their response.
- We believe their judgements of our actions to be accurate.
- We change our actions to match their assessment.
        ...and then the cycle repeats itself.

Grandma Thompson was one person who had healthy self-esteem. What others thought of her, mattered little to her. She followed those values she felt were important - like hard work, honesty and making life an adventure. She was as comfortable riding at the bow of an old row boat, or pitching straw, as she was dining from fine China with elite society.

At Sarah Jane's wedding, Grandma Thompson was dressed in all her finery, and young Bobby offered her a bite of the dainty square he was eating. He held it up to Grandma Thompson's mouth. Just as she sank her teeth into the square, he feared that she was going to take too big a bite. He quickly withdrew the square, complete with Grandma Thompson's dentures. Unfazed, Grandma Thompson reached for the dentures and placed them back in her mouth. She laughed and hugged Bobby, telling him, "it is so much fun to be a grandma!"

Many of us would have been devastated by the same experience. Grandma Thompson had learned not to sweat the small stuff. She had learned that when you laugh at life, it laughs with you. What's more, many adults shatter the self-esteem of a child when they ineffectively deal with their own insecurities. It is very important to see the humor in our own inadequacies, and to recognize that embarrassing things happen to everyone, at one time or another.

Unless we are fortunate enough to be surrounded by healthy, supportive people, this cyclical appraisal of our self-worth is the sure path to loss of self-esteem. Failing to believe in ourselves, and adopting the often erroneous judgements of other people, is usually self-defeating.

The most important opinion of you is your own opinion: believe in yourself. The process of self-discovery can increase the belief in oneself. We are the managers of our own lives. We need to

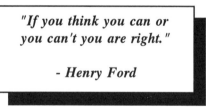

"If you think you can or you can't you are right."

- Henry Ford

know what the manager expects. Yet, so often we fail to take the time to get to know our own selves. We ignore our own needs for nurturing and love.

You must love yourself before you can love others. When you love yourself, you are not limited to a reality which is created by living for the approval of others. If you have had a dysfunctional childhood, you need to spend even more time learning to love yourself.

The self-fulfilling prophecy plays a role in your self-image. What you think you are, is what you become. This long understood philosophy is one of the underlying premises of this entire book.

However, it goes right back to your beliefs. If you think or act like a failure, you will become one. If you think or act like a success, you will become one. If there is no change in your beliefs, there will be no change in your actions: no change results in no change.

Healthy self-esteem means having the confidence to celebrate our individuality. Self-doubt leads to doing things merely to impress others. Erroneous beliefs can erode our self-confidence. Faulty beliefs must be changed. It is equally important to have congruence between our perception of our actual self, our desired self, and our presenting self. The greater the gap between the way we present ourselves to others, and our perception of ourselves, the more we will feel turmoil. Confusion and conflict are not conducive to the growth of self-esteem.

It is not always the criticism or actions of others that diminishes our self-esteem. It is a misconception that self put-downs are an indication of modesty. We can put ourselves down physically, sexually, or by denying our creative talents, criticizing ourselves for not measuring up to family expectations, berating our intelligence, or ridiculing our relationship skills.

Time out:
How does your self-esteem measure up? Are there ways you put yourself down?

Redefining your Identity

Self-concept is like a mirror, reflecting ourselves as we believe we appear. It is subjective and can be improved. We can choose to play an active role in initiating this change. Self-esteem is the belief in self, based on this image.

Self-concept and the subsequent development of self-esteem are based in part on our assessment of our personal worth. Frequent,

> *"Every person needs recognition.*
> *It is expressed cogently by the lad who says,*
> *"Mother, let's play darts. I'll throw the darts and you say 'Wonderful'."*
>
> *- M. Dale Baughman*

inaccurate interpretation of personal failures leads to low self-esteem. Interpreting failure, as a sometimes necessary step in the process of personal growth, is a healthier choice. Believing failure to be a measurement of one's personal worth, is inaccurate and self-defeating.

Our image of self is dependent on self-respect. Respect is earned. It cannot be purchased. When we engage in self-care, nurture our inner self, and meet our emotional needs we develop self-respect. Invalidating our feelings by ignoring them and by telling ourselves our feelings are unimportant, causes a deeper hurt than if others do it to us. Too often, we expect others to treat us better than we treat ourselves.

The respect of others, particularly those closest to us, is important. We earn it by honoring them emotionally, by showing unconditional love, and by keeping commitments. Too often, we may assume our partner or our children, will respect us more if we are generous and if we buy them expensive gifts. Many parents do this, in an attempt to improve their relationship with their teenager.

Bringing out the credit card can just be saying, "I don't have time for you. I don't know what you need or want, and I am not willing to listen long enough to find out." Children of all ages need validation, unconditional love, and parents who are willing to communicate.

Often, communicating needs to be 70 percent listening and 30 percent talking, with a total suspension of judgement. As children reach their late teens, they try their wings and need your emotional support.

Additionally, self-esteem is based on the opinions others have of us. If the opinion is from a person who is perceived to be more competent and qualified, more weight will be attached to their comments. This can be changed in two ways.

First, reevaluate whose comments you are going to accept as relevant. This can be done by objectively assessing the perception you have of needing approval from this person. Low

> *"Most of the shadows in this life are caused by standing in one's own sunshine."*
>
> *-Anonymous*

self-esteem can lead to an inferiority complex. Believing oneself to be of less value, or ability, results in a heavy emotional load. It is like being with someone you dislike, only you cannot escape - because the someone is you! There isn't anyone who deserves this kind of prison sentence.

Low self-esteem is usually the result of accepting the judgments of some controlling, critical authority figure from the past. Understanding the source and putting it in perspective is a powerful step in taking back control of one's life. Love yourself: love yourself unconditionally. The emotional pain of carrying a negative image of oneself is a barrier to personal growth.

Second, you can determine how you are going to perceive and react to the comments. Taking them personally increases their effect. If you see the comment as constructive feedback about a behavior - attaching it to the behavior rather than using it as a measurement of your worth - you will be more able to put it in a neutral perspective.

The judgement of others only affects us if it is at least moderately consistent with our own opinion about ourselves. Therefore, by taking the responsibility to see ourselves in a positive light, we neutralize the negative comments of others.

Selecting peer groups and friends who support you is important. The important part here is 'selecting,' not allowing it to happen by chance. Good relationships are the result of intentional relationship building techniques. Chapter 8, **Shared Meaning,** deals more extensively with relationship building.

Time out:

Are the people whose opinions you value providing you with unconditional support, or are they undermining your self-concept? How does your opinion of significant others in your life reinforce or sabotage their self-concept?

Chapter 7

"I Think...Therefore I Am!"

> *"There are two ways to slide through life;*
> *to believe everything, or to doubt everything.*
> *Both ways save us from thinking. "*
>
> *- A. Korzybski*

Quest for Knowledge

Life is a quest for knowledge. By nature, humans seek to: understand the unknown; explain the unexplained; unravel the mysteries of the universe; and understand the mysteries of human behavior. Humans strive to find ways of predicting the unexpected, to improve the ways we interact with our environment, and with one another. Our quest for knowledge is ongoing, and should continue throughout our life span.

Knowledge increases accountability. For example it is difficult or unfair to hold people responsible for damaging the environment, if they are not aware that what they are doing is harmful. That does not absolve the responsibility to acquire the knowledge necessary to make informed decisions.

Obviously all the years that society has spent destroying the eco-systems has not lead to any blissful situation. Some people believe "ignorance is bliss." Those who buy into this faulty paradigm, are paralyzed by an unwillingness to look beyond themselves. They live in the prison of limited reality.

Learning is like change, there is a risk attached. As with change, there is a loss and a gain. The loss may be the need to let go of old beliefs or ways of doing things. It may be a loss of our innocence. It may lead to having to admit that we were wrong - about what we thought, or did. The gain that is experienced can be in the form of greater freedom, new opportunities, increased challenges, and/or increased accountability.

The voice of our ego may pose the question, "why would I want increased challenges?" This is caused by a desire to maintain our existing state. Accepting responsibility means confronting change. Although it is irrational, many people are as afraid of success as they are of failure. What would happen if you were suddenly incredibly successful?

> *"Education does not mean teaching people to know what they do not know; it means teaching them to behave as they do not behave."*
>
> *-John Ruskin*

As for challenges, our human existence is dependent on challenges. However, there needs to be a balance. Lack of challenge can lead to boredom, and boredom can make you sick. The problem is real - it is a primary factor in build-up of stress, and in skyrocketing medical costs. On the other end of the continuum, too much of the wrong kind of challenges can cause stress and also make you sick. The answer lies in balancing out the challenges, and ensuring that they allow for a sense of fulfilment.

As for accountability, humans thrive when they know that others can count on them. We all like to feel needed. We need to feel like we have a talent or ability that makes us useful and that makes a difference. When we know we are accountable, it builds our self-esteem, and empowers us to take greater risks.

A day in which we do not learn anything new is a day wasted. Time is a commodity that cannot be purchased, and is non-redeemable. Once you have spent the day, you cannot relive it. In our quest for knowledge, it is important that our learning be without boundaries, and lifelong.

Education versus Learning

We all know people who are well educated, but not very wise. What is the difference between learning and education? Education usually takes place in a more formal setting, and involves another person who teaches the subject matter. Learning can take place in a formal environment, or without a teacher and in a very informal setting. Education can take place without learning taking place.

It is possible to assimilate information doled out by a teacher, and not learn to think creatively or critically. This is more likely to occur where testing is done based on rote, or the word for word repetition of the teacher's instruction. Requiring the learner to use critical analysis, evaluation, and application of knowledge is a better indication of the student's understanding.

Learning can take place when we encounter a new situation, or through experience. The greater our awareness, the more likely we are to learn from the environment, and from our experience. I learned by experience in grade three, that digging up the roots of a peanut plant doesn't speed growth. I was so anxious to see if there were any peanuts that I repeatedly dug up the plant! Not only did it result in crop failure, it

> *"The teacher is one who makes two ideas grow where only one grew before."*
>
> *- Elbert Hubbard*

finally killed the plant. Experience can be a harsh teacher. Nevertheless, experience is frequently the teacher when we need to learn patience.

Two people can have the same experience and one may not learn a thing, while the other may achieve a powerful new insight. If we are present centered, aware and watching for opportunities to learn, and if we approach each experience with an open mind, we will learn much more.   This applies to education also. Young or old, we need to be open to learn, to think critically, and creatively. If we aspire to understand the implications of the material we are learning from many different perspectives, we will learn much more.

It has been long understood that people should sample disciplines that are different from their core curriculum. Most degree granting institutions require that to get a sciences degree, at least a few arts courses must be completed, and vice versa. This is because we become more balanced in our perspective if we can understand the different philosophies and disciplines.

For example, the accountant who has taken courses in sociology will better understand the sociological impact of the numbers he or she works with from day to day. We become more capable of making moral and ethical decisions when we can understand the different perspectives. We learn to understand others, even when we do not agree.

Learning leads to wisdom when we suspend personal judgements based on differences in opinion. Our ability to learn from ourselves and others can assist us in working as part of a team.

"University Extension is meant for those for whom religion is intended; for those for whom life, liberty, and the pursuit of happiness is intended. It is meant to help the ignorant who desire knowledge - that they may learn wisely; to reveal to the half-educated the insufficiency of their knowledge; to arouse intellectual sluggards; to stimulate those who are in the right way; to bring questions to the hearts of the self-satisfied. "

- American Society for the Extension of University Teaching, 1910

Learning New Skills

Skills are knowledge with a practical application. The level of skill we can acquire in a particular field is limitless. Becoming competent in a variety of fields can serve us well.

Constantly attempting to learn new skills, enables us to acquire them more quickly. People who stay in one job for many years can encounter a very rough road if they suddenly find themselves needing to change jobs. It is even more difficult if they have not actively pursued additional training. It is always beneficial to have a *profession* and a marketable *hobby.* Sometimes a hobby can lead to a very profitable business. No matter what our profession is, it is good to have an alternative to fall back on.

> *"Human beings find less rest in idleness than in a change of occupation... just try it. Instead of collapsing in an easy chair, try tackling your hobby. Or write that neglected letter, or help Johnny build that radio receiving set. Activity-especially creative activity-is far better recreation than loafing."*
>
> *-Gardner Hunting*

Gone are the days when you worked for a company for forty-five years and then received your golden pocket watch or engraved plaque. Most people change jobs, and/or careers completely, three or more times in a life time.

I have recently heard of an electrical engineer who is becoming a pastor...a nurse who has become an airline pilot...and a doctor who quit medicine to become a restaurant owner. These are voluntary changes. Immigrants may face career difficulties because of other choices they have made. They may find themselves driving cabs, or patching pavement, even though they were doctors or lawyers in their homeland.

The tenacity and willingness to take risks, can enable displaced people to initiate the changes and rise to the top. Sometimes the person who appears to have the least opportunities becomes the most successful. Look at your high school grad class. How many of the ones who seemed to exhibit little chance of success, have become successful? How many who seemed to "have it made" during high school, have shown little initiative or success in their adult lives?

Attitude determines more than means, when predicting success. Two beetles fell in an ounce of cream. One thought it was too hard swimming in the thick cream, and sank to the bottom and drowned. The other struggled to keep swimming, and was found floating on a lump of butter. We can face the challenge and initiate a change, or we can allow irrational fears to cause us to sink and drown.

Learning Without Boundaries

When we limit what we are willing to learn, we limit our reality. Often we assume we know enough. How often have you started a job, assuming you knew what you were doing, only for it to take far longer than if you gathered the information first?

Instruction manuals, for example, no matter how boring, are printed for a reason. Attempting to assemble a bicycle after reading the first and last page of "How to Assemble a Bicycle" can result in many left-over parts and no brakes! Short cuts are often not worth taking, and are an illusion created by an unwillingness to accept help from others.

It is useful to explore different avenues of learning and different sources. Learn to think critically. Until I attended university, I believed that statistics were valid information which could not be disputed. Now I understand that statistics can be skewed to tell any story the statistician decides to tell. That is not a slam against statisticians. Merely the bias  that the person doing the survey has, is enough to distort the information even when controls are in place. Sometimes the controls are not adequate, and the information is distorted. We all have the tendency to screen things and see things from our own perspectives.

"New learning is a temporary loss of security."

- Madeline Hunter

As our perspectives broaden, through acquiring additional information, we recognize that there is usually more than one right answer. The world no longer appears to be made up of right and wrong, or black and white answers. Perfectly valid perspectives are as varied as the colors of the rainbow. Black and white are the extremes caused by reflecting or absorbing all of the colors in the spectrum. Black *muddies* and white *washes out* the clarity of any other color you mix it with.

Our quest for knowledge has the most meaning when we suspend our need to be right by making others appear wrong. It is not necessary for us to be right. It is more important for us to be aware. Awareness requires a willingness to listen and understand the perspective of others. Wisdom is demonstrated when people are content to know what their personal truth is, without prejudice for others with different opinions, and without feeling any need to obtain consensus from others.

> *"Let your interests be as wide as possible, and let your reactions to the things and persons that interest you be as far as possible friendly rather than hostile."*
>
> *- Bertrand Russell*

Wisdom and maturity come from recognizing that living one's personal truth requires neither our conformity to others, nor others conforming to our beliefs. It cannot co-exist with malice or jealousy. The uninterrupted flow of creation can only benefit from our cognitive potential when we celebrate our similarities and honor our individual differences in our relationships with others.

Time out:
What are some of the things that muddy or wash out the clarity of your perception? Have you included planned learning into your personal Action Plan?

Chapter 8

Shared Meaning

> *"Whatever you can do, or dream that you can, begin it. Boldness has genius, power and magic in it."*
>
> *- Johann W. von Goethe*

Social Need

One of our human needs is for interaction with other individuals and groups. Extensive studies have examined social behavior, structures and interaction. Society can be defined in terms of these social structures and/or in terms of people's perceptions of the social environment. Over the past century various sociologists have developed frameworks and theories which can help us better understand the forces and influences of society on our individual behaviors.

Emile Durkhiem believed we could not understand the behavior of the individual, without looking at the properties of society. Max Weber believed we could not understand others unless we had "walked a mile in their moccasins." He believed people developed their perceptions by thinking through the logic of situations. Karl Marx stated that separating the capitalist business owners from those working for wages, results in social inequalities. George Herbert Mead believed our sense of self emerges through social interaction. Irving Goffman perceived life to be as a theater, with humans acting out displays.

These sociologists describe varying philosophies. Taking the time to study the works of these and other sociologists can enable you to more clearly develop your personal philosophy. The point of view you take will influence your interactions with others.

We are a product of the society in which we live, however the reverse is also true. Our society is a product of the people who comprise it. The society we are born into already exists. However, we have our individual roles to play in transforming it. Often people feel they are powerless. They feel compelled to conform to commonly held principles and values - or norms. Conformity is an illusion. Society has no collective mind, and for every one person you please there are a few others whom you will displease. Our responsibility is to ourselves. When we do what is best for ourselves, and do it with integrity, the benefit will ripple out to others.

Social problems affect our health, relationships and ability to cope in the business community. It is all encompassing. The factors that affect one part of our lives ultimately affects all other parts of our lives. The communities we live in are full of problems which affect us as individuals. Do we have a responsibility to influence society in an attempt to address these problems?

Just like personal change comes from the inside - society also changes from the inside out. Any change must begin with individuals. As each individual changes, it ripples out to an observable difference when we look at society.

Too often, people adapt to the status quo, rather than actively choosing their own values. We all know our communities are less than ideal. Our school systems and family lives do not prepare us. In fact, these structures often do the reverse, crippling us mentally and emotionally, making us less able to cope.

The structures intended to lead to a functional society are faltering. It is evident in our divorce statistics, crime rates, suicide rates and unemployment statistics. The United States and Canada are among the countries with the highest use of antidepressant prescription drugs. Under-developed countries have much lower incidence of suicide and lower use of mood altering prescription drugs. The reason is likely to be lifestyle related. Do the drugs work? If so, what would the North American suicide rate be without them? What does it say about the North American life style?

Community

Many people, particularly in large cities, have very little sense of community. Those who complain, are the same people who are not actively involved in the community. The

> *"No great improvements in the lot of mankind are possible, until a great change takes place in the fundamental institution of their modes of thought."*
>
> *-John Stewart Mill*

tendency to isolate ourselves from our neighbors can contribute to the lack of safety and harmony in the community.

Often, grassroots movements initiate change within communities. The recycling movement demonstrates something good that started as a grassroots movement. A few individuals initiated the change. Gradually, others adopted the idea. Now most people consider recycling a socially responsible thing to do. We can only affect change when we believe we can make choices, and only when we decide to take action to make the choices a reality.

The Power of One

We cannot change all the decaying social ails in our community. That does not mean we are not responsible for repairing and maintaining those which most directly affect us personally. It calls for us to be more responsible, and more proactive. When we have responded to our personal needs - we can then move forward and have a greater influence in society.

All collective changes are initiated by individual or small group efforts. Society does not have, or exercise a collective will. Society does not exist without, or *a priori* (before) the individual. It has no behavior, except the behavior of the individuals who constitute it.

When the passion of our lives is fueling our actions, that passion becomes evident to others, and our lives can inspire them to take action. Social change comes from individual change, and the only part you can play is to facilitate personal change. However, one person with a dream can make a big difference.

Examples are Martin Luther King, and Mahatma Ghandi. Consider the impact of King's speech, "**I Have a Dream**." Consider the effect of Ghandi's great work. He had a vision, and his passion made it a reality.

It is possible to change one's life very radically. First, it requires in depth examination of the personal beliefs we allow to run our lives. Then it requires changing faulty beliefs, vision, commitment, and changing powerless behavior into powerful behavior.

Once the process begins, it becomes easier. Even if you are consumed by a dysfunctional downward spiral, it is possible for you to soar with the eagles. If your life is already functioning fairly well, this process will enable you to reach new heights.

The beauty of personal growth is that it is endless. The more we grow, the more wonderful the opportunities are, that manifest themselves to us. The speed with which change occurs in your life is a product of three factors: your passion, your willingness to do the homework and your starting point.

We all have challenges that are unique to us as individuals. The truth is, eclectically tuned in individuals have more opportunities than they can ever use. The rewards will soon become added fuel to fire up your passion. You can soon reach a point where those around you will wonder how they too can catch your enthusiasm. However, it is not like a virus, which you get from someone else. Each individual is the master of his or her own destiny.

I believe the seeds of passion and vision are in every one of us - they just need a chance to be nourished and cultivated. Passion and vision may be like seeds laying dormant. The husks that encase the seed need to be removed, so the seeds can germinate and start to grow.

Culture and Ethnicity

Taking a multicultural perspective can increase tolerance and increase our ability to understand others. It can enable individuals to choose traits from each culture, which they would like to incorporate in their own life plan. There is no perfect culture - each has strengths and weaknesses. The key is to recognize these and learn from the strengths of others.

Cultural norms do not spring from a political beginning, however they may be influenced by political definitions. Whether the individual agrees or disagrees with government policies, these policies ultimately affect the lives of individual citizens. Lawmaking tends to be reactive, rather than proactive. With increasing deficits, policies often reflect an economic decision, rather than a decision for the benefit of the public. Sometimes, vocal groups have more power and influence than the popular vote or the ruling political party. Laws usually follow rather than precede change.

While democratic governments attempt to meet the needs of citizens, there is no simple answer. If the majority rules, then the minority is not living in an environment where the government represents its needs or desires. Even those who are supporters of the political party in power, may find many of their desires are not met. These are complex problems that confront our political leaders. Criticism and apathy do not contribute to solutions. So, how can democracy be redefined or how can democracy address the needs of the individual more effectively?

Role Models, Mentors and Coaches

Some people who have passed through tragedy, manage to make a marvellous recovery, and go on to be mentors to others. Others seem to fold and give up, over the loss of a job. What makes the difference? People who survive great adversity can choose to go on to become great role models to others. Often they have spirits that are more alive than some of those around them who have had comparatively few problems.

One cannot attribute happiness to the abundance of possessions, or fairly judge one person to be more capable than the other. By the time we reach adulthood, we know about 4,000 people. We can readily identify the ones who influenced our lives most. Everyone should consciously select a few role models. It is a way of benefiting from those within our society who have meaningful knowledge and experiences to share with us.

When you choose to mentor another person, it calls you to accountability. Your sense of responsibility to that person results in you being more aware of the choices you are making, and the impact of those choices. It is accepting a call to be the best that you can be. Mentoring is an opportunity to give without expecting a return. Focus on what you can give, rather than what you can get.

Unlike a mentor or role model, a coach fills a more active role. A Personal Success Coach is a consultant who helps get you on track and keeps you on track. The coach guides a client through the process of discovering his or her passion, then assists the client in making it a reality in the most effective and painless way possible. It is about supporting and guiding individuals to achieve and clarify both their personal and professional goals. Like a sports coach, the Personal Success Coach teaches techniques, assigns exercises, identifies barriers to success and motivates. It is an ongoing process.

Hiring a Personal Success Coach is a trend that is becoming increasingly popular. The culture of business is changing so rapidly that many managers need help with the transitions that confront them. People who have spent many years heading up departments feel like their jobs have lost meaning.

Similarly, a person who has been successful in business may seek assistance to bring his or her life into balance. High achievers often come to the realization that it is costing them in other areas of their lives. Redefining success, and then assisting the person in identifying and initiating realistic and meaningful changes, restores balance.

Individuals undergoing career transitions, starting new businesses or in careers involving sales, find coaching an asset to their progress. Coaching provides the missing link between attending motivational seminars and achievement. Unless our good intentions are put into action, change will not occur. The weekly, one-on-one sessions empower the individual to stay on track.

> *"If a man doesn't know what port he is heading for, no wind is favorable to him."*
>
> *-Seneca*

Relationships

Relationships play a major role in the needs of our social self. The connection between ourselves and others is founded on our ability to act and interact in a way that creates shared meaning. Healthy relationships are based on communication, understanding, equality, respect, exchange, reciprocity, and desire for common good.

Our interactions with others are less personal in the workplace than in other situations. It is important to establish our own boundaries in the workplace. Usually, the more junior the position, in the workplace, the less equality there will be in the relationship. However, supervisors still need to show respect for the individuality of junior employees. No employee deserves to be invalidated. The workplace is discussed in depth in Chapter 9, **Making a Difference.**

Some people believe personal or family relationships can thrive with a dominant partner and a subordinate partner. The dominant partner often controls the other. That is not power, it is manipulation or domination. Power is taking the action necessary to change our own dreams (visions) into realities. When we can do this successfully, we see the difference, and we will encourage others to create their own visions, and to make their own dreams become realities. When we change our visions into realities, we become accountable, and others can trust our word.

Power is the ability to do and act. It is the ability to change intention into reality. Effective relationship building behaviors include clear communication, trust building, clear intentions, commitment and integrity.

Communication

A historian and a psychologist were sitting in a park. The historian said "My wife is too fond of history. When she gets mad at me, she becomes historical."

> *"The greatest compliment that was ever paid to me was when one asked me what I thought, and attended to my answer."*
>
> *- Henry David Thoreau*

"I think you are working too hard, you meant hysterical, didn't you?" the psychologist responded.

"No," replied the historian, "I mean historical - she always refers to disagreements that happened twenty years ago."

Often our communication skills are at their worst when we converse with those we care most about. Unclear messages result in misunderstandings. Interpersonal understanding requires clear messages, in marriages, friendships and the workplace. Ineffective communication in a marriage can lead to an unexpected communication from the spouse's lawyer. In the workplace, it causes disgruntled customers and fellow employees. It may lead to an unpleasant conversation in the boss's office and an unexpected pink slip.

Powerful people are able to express themselves clearly. We need to seek to understand others and then to make ourselves understood. Too often we assume others understand.

"Why didn't you say something before now?"

"I did, I told you four times. You just didn't listen."

"I was listening, I just didn't hear what you said."

"I thought you understood."

Sounds familiar doesn't it? Awareness of the reasons why misunderstandings occur, increases our ability to avoid them.

Communication is a complex activity, and is influenced by many things. Words are merely symbols. Often the symbol means something different to one person than it does to another. I recently met a woman from England who was on holiday in Toronto. She phoned her son in Vancouver and informed him that so far her vacation had been wonderful. She told him she had met a fine gentleman with a bathtub and that they had been spending the evenings together in it.

The son gasped, "Mother, I was just going to bed to have a good sleep. Now I am going to lay awake all night worrying about you!" The mother was calling a hot tub, a bathtub. Individual interpretations of a message are seldom the same.

Added to this challenge are many other factors that affect our ability to get the message. Environmental noise, or noise in the surrounding area produced by other people talking, radios, televisions, or machinery, can alter our ability to physically hear the message. Our minds constantly play "tapes" or messages from our subconscious. Personal concerns, or other information can cause us to be preoccupied. This internal dialogue or 'self-talk' can alter our perception. Pre-conceived ideas about the intentions of the person sending the message may make us defensive, and as a result, we can block out parts of the message.

Clear communication requires concise language. Using big words or complex wording can lead to ambiguity, which does nothing to build understanding in a relationship.

Some of the most powerless words in the English language are BUT, CAN'T, SHOULD, and TRY. When the word 'but' is used, the entire preceding statement is cancelled. Here is an example: "I want to help you with your homework, but I have to repair my boat." The person making the statement really does not want to help the other person, because if the desire was to help, the boat would get repaired some other time. The word 'but' cancels the first part of the statement.

"I can't" is the most negative statement we can make. It really means "I won't" or "I don't want to." It is an attempt to deny personal responsibility for taking action. Sometimes people go one step farther, and use "I can't" in a statement that names someone else as the reason why they can't. For example, "I can't go because my partner is expecting me to stay home this evening." This is either allowing the other person the control, or denying any responsibility for a personal decision. Either way, it is not good communication.

A native American once told me the word "should" does not exist in any of the aboriginal languages used by native Americans. They believe it needs to be replaced with either "need" or "want." If you try this out, you will find it is true. The things you say you *should* do are either things you *want* to do or things you *need* to do. It is better to be honest with ourselves and others, and change the word *should* to *need* or *want* as appropriate.

Using the word *try*, suggests the possibility of accomplishing the task while it leaves a way out without any consequences. *Try* is an example of tentative language. *Try* offers no commitment. Effective communicators avoid words such as *maybe, sometime, probably* and similar words because these words lead to misunderstandings.

Effective listening is vital. Allow yourself to really listen, without interrupting or distracting the speaker. It validates the other person and allows them to carry their thought to completion. A willingness to listen leads to a better relationship. Individual needs and wants are more easily met when there is a clearer understanding.

Time out:
What are some of the challenges you face in communicating? What words do you use to absolve your personal responsibility? Are you a good listener?

Trust Building

Powerful people do what they say they are going to do. Keeping commitments is an indispensable tool for building relationships. Being accountable leads to trustworthiness. Sometimes, inadvertently, we have damaged the level of trust in a relationship because of something we have said or done. It must be re-established. Trust is necessary for growth. It is built through risk and confirmation; and is destroyed through risk and disconfirming responses.

Financial institutions frequently have trust departments. The client takes his money from under the mattress and deposits it in an account in hopes of earning a good return. The financial institution manages the funds. If stocks go up - so does the client's trust. If stocks go down - so does the client's trust.

The unseasoned investor brings in a deposit. The market plummets and - guess what? - the investor withdraws the funds. Then the market starts to improve, and the investor brings in money again, believing there is money to be made. Once again the investor buys high - and the market drops. The investor may withdraw - and never trust the financial institution again. Money under the mattress will never generate a revenue, and hearts filled with distrust will never feel love.

It works the same in relationships and in careers. Trust has to be earned. It starts with small deposits. When you make promises or commitments, and keep them, others recognize it. It leads to a willingness to work toward mutual goals. Having a team spirit and honoring our commitments increases our accountability.

There is a risk that the commitment (or deposit) you make to the trust account -- is not going to be noticed, appreciated, or reciprocated. However, unless you take that chance, you cannot move forward in the relationship. Relationships are based on giving and receiving. After all, there is only one question that you need to ask to determine if you are a greedy or giving person. "Do I give without expecting to receive?" If you don't, you are greedy, and perhaps others have reason not to trust you. Often it is when we give, not expecting to receive back, that we receive the greatest personal rewards.

Team Building

Many times, relationships rely on team work. I heard of a woman who volunteered to help at a charity rummage sale. She prided herself in that she had sold twenty-three coats off the rack next to her table, by noon. The coordinator's response was different. "Good heavens," she gasped, "those coats belonged to the volunteers." The mandate obviously was not clear.

Understanding the dynamics of team building, and becoming a team player, enhances family, the community and workplace relationships. Employers often find people who have played team sports bring a cooperative attitude to the workplace.

A team is a group of people who, by informal or formal agreement, interact to accomplish mutual goals through interdependent activities. Mandate and structure need to be defined, so the people involved understand who is and who is not part of the Action Plan. The members need a clear understanding of their individual responsibilities. Each member's skills are recognized and utilized for mutual gain. The membership assembles to accomplish a common mandate. The membership may dissolve if the project is completed.

Healthy teams do not require any of the individuals to sacrifice their own identity, or conform to principles, beliefs or values that violate the individual's autonomy. Healthy teams celebrate the individuality of the members. The combined skills of the membership provide a synergy enabling the team to accomplish more than is possible by individual efforts. Team members share a commitment to a common vision while maintaining their individuality.

Unhealthy groups often have autocratic leadership. Anytime group members stop thinking for themselves, it is a danger signal. The sense of oneness in an unhealthy group may attract people who feel insecure, or who lack the confidence to express their own opinions. Cults and gangs fall into this category. These groups become havens for a myriad of problems when the group leader controls the actions of the group members and the members fail to think individually. Maintaining awareness and examining the philosophy of the group can help identify unhealthy environments.

Time out:

How recently have you sat with the members of your team and discussed the mandate? Do the teams you are a part of play on a level playing field?

Family

The concept of family is culturally created, and varies greatly from ethnic group to ethnic group even within North America. Family structure has changed as arranged marriages have been replaced with love marriages, and the Industrial Revolution and urbanization changed our entire social structure.

While it may appear that urbanization has reduced the interdependence between the nuclear and extended family, this varies greatly even within our culture. Inter-relationship frequently provides a reciprocal-exchange system. The needs of one part of the extended family are met by the resources of the other parts of the family, and vice versa. Both the definition of family and its structure varies greatly. It is necessary to create for ourselves an environment that enables us to find meaning.

Many families are strongly united networks that support one another in good and bad times. The members know who to turn to for help in various situations, and that they can depend on assistance. These types of relationships are very valuable. Those who have them understand the value of resolving conflicts before they escalate, and the value of clear communication.

Individuals see themselves as contributors to the harmony of the entire unit. They value family ties and are willing to work together to help one another out. Often they pay little attention to what they are going to get in return for the contributions they make. However, many people do not come from families like this.

Frequently, divorce fragments the family and one of the former partners may find him or her self rejected by in-laws or relatives. This becomes increasingly complicated when there are children involved. This however, is not the only time relatives may attempt to interfere with personal choices. Decisions to cohabit in a trial marriage, or as a permanent alternative to marriage, may cause a reaction among family members. Choice of partners or lifestyle may also cause conflict.

Some families can be very supportive in difficult times. Others can be a hindrance to personal growth, and in some cases, can be a shattering influence on self-esteem. It depends greatly on the dynamics of the extended family relationship.

People who go through divorce often experience feelings of guilt. This guilt can result in devastating emotional turmoil which is undeserved and unnecessary. Sometimes it is self-inflicted because of personal commitment to life-long marriage. While it is a wholesome belief the sad but true reality is it often does not work out that way. When additional pressure is inflicted by family and friends to save the deteriorating marriage, agony is often prolonged instead of prevented.

The challenge we all face is to accept the opinions of other family members, and to show unconditional love. When we operate from this perspective, we forego any temptation to control others. This leads to increased harmony. It makes it easier for the individual members to create a meaningful reality.

A difficult choice can confront those who do not have a supportive immediate or extended family. Divorce is more widely accepted than it once was. However, those who experience it invariably find some of their friends and family are quick to criticize and pass judgement. This can be devastating to the self-esteem of a person who worked very hard at the marriage.

When a person, who has been controlled by others in the family, takes control of his or her own life, it can lead to family conflict. The other person who has had the control does not want to lose it. If this occurs, clearly explain your need to have control of your own choices, without interference from other family members. If there is a continued unwillingness to stop interfering, reducing interaction with the family may be the only alternative. If this is the only choice, it becomes very important for the individual to develop a strong supportive network of friends.

Strong social ties, family or otherwise have been given credit for reducing a person's need for counselling. The support of friends and family plays a significant role in enabling us to deal effectively with our own problems. We need a social safety-net, not as a source of free advice, but rather because of a need to hear ourselves talk about the problem aloud. Talking about the problem forces us to define it. This often helps us find the solution we need. It can sometimes prevent us from making foolish mistakes. A wrong choice may seem quite logical until you express it verbally.

Time out:
Is your family supportive? What resources do you have if your family is not supportive?

Love Relationships

The assumption that love is enough to hold partners together is probably the most erroneous assumption in the territory of relationship management. Love relationships take two, working together toward mutually agreeable goals. It doesn't matter how hard one partner tries to make it work if the other partner is not involved in the process, it will never work. Too many of us wake up one day to realize there is no relationship - it had died long ago. Relationships are not latent, they change and evolve.

> *"The finer qualities of our nature, like the bloom on fruits, can only be preserved by the most delicate handling, yet we do not treat ourselves nor one another thus tenderly."*
>
> *- Henry David Thoreau*

Intimate relationships are difficult. There are numerous conflicting needs and desires in operation at all times. While partners long for harmony and connectedness, they also struggle with their individual needs and desires for autonomy. Partners want for a sense of security and stability; and also want to maintain spontaneity and novelty. The relationship is fed by the gender based differences and at the same time struggles to balance the needs, desires, and viewpoints of masculine and feminine identities. Partners recognize the need for openness - a freedom to self-disclose, yet this is contrasted with individual needs and desires for privacy.

Having an Action Plan and initiating changes can make a significant difference to a relationship. But...it takes two. Both partners have to be equally committed to making changes and sustaining the union. Often, they can be achieved quite simply by choosing to follow some of the following techniques:

- More time spent together in present centered awareness.
- Time spent where nothing but each other matters.
- Demonstrating the qualities of caring, honesty, and loyalty.
- Creating an environment where disclosure and communication can occur without threat of criticism.
- Learning to listen and listening to learn.
- Celebrating similarities and honoring diversity relating to opinions and abilities.
- Applying the 'Golden Rule,' (treating others as you want them to treat you).
- Honoring personal space and understanding one another's needs for intimacy and understanding.

> *"The face is the mirror of the mind, and eyes without speaking confess the secrets of the heart"*
>
> *- St. Jerome*

We must remember that each partner is also changing. Partners must integrate the personal growth of each other in such a way as to honor the individual and celebrate the union.

A cat sitting outside the mousehole is an obvious danger signal to the mouse. Not all signals of danger are as easy to identify. A sleeping cat can be deceiving. The cheese sitting on a mouse trap is inanimate. The mouse may assume it can't be of any danger. It is important to be able to recognize the danger signals that occur.

Trouble begins when a couple is not able to negotiate a balance between the relationship needs and individual needs of each partner. Behaviors that are more passive are just as likely to be signals of serious problems as more confrontational behaviors. We are less likely to clue in to the discontent of the other partner, if the behavior is non-confrontational. These responses can include:

- Demonstrating ill-at-ease body language.
- Changing the topic, or leaving the room.
- Sarcasm used in humor, especially when it is in reference to the partner or the partner's actions.
- Showing even mild contempt.
- Withdrawal: either mental or physical.

Often, when things are not going well the approach we use to correct the problem is equally ineffective. It may be as ineffective as the cat who eats the cheese and sits outside the mousehole with baited breath. The cat hopes his luck will improve. If we depend on luck to change our personal situations, we are no smarter than the cat. Conversely, attending programs or counselling, to develop relationship skills is a proactive and effective approach.

If the behaviors listed above are occuring, they are red flags which need to alert partners to their relationship problems. These characteristics signal that the problems have escalated to a point where immediate action is needed for survival. If the issues are not resolved at this point, the relationship will stagnate.

When the relationship becomes too difficult to endure, even couples who have held strong commitments to life long marriage will begin to avoid one another. At this point, the damage is usually irreversible, and the inevitable will happen sooner or later. Delaying the inevitable only adds to the unpleasantness of the separation. It can lead to a divorce process that is long and drawn out and filled with bitter jabs at each other.

The more dysfunctional the relationship is, or was, the more difficult it is to separate and remain on civil terms. Delaying the ending of an unhappy and unhealthy relationship, only results in greater difficulty putting your life back together. It shatters self-esteem, makes ties to extended family more difficult, and is disastrous for children.

Divorce statistics influence us to believe that there are more problems in marriages now than there were fifty years ago. I do not believe that is true. I believe that women, in particular, remained in dead relationships, because they did not see any way out. Although women still lag behind men in earning power, today most women are aware they can make it on their own. Even if it is difficult, it is better than staying in a dysfunctional relationship.

It cannot be emphasized enough that good relationships do not happen by chance. Therefore, it is something the partners can choose to make work. Communicate your needs to one another, develop an Action Plan, and initiate the changes that will keep your relationship healthy.

Don't wait until the relationship is in trouble, and don't stop working at it when it seems to be doing well. It is assumed that as long as the relationship is moderately healthy - and as long as it is functioning better than some of the others around you - you are okay. Unfortunately, dysfunctional relationships are so common, we assume that it is just a fact of life. We lower our expectations and ignore the possibilities of having an optimum relationship. Accept the challenge to move beyond mediocrity to excellence.

Time out:
What actions can you take to improve the relationships in your life? What are some of the things that make the relationships work well? What needs to be addressed?

Chapter 9

Making a Difference

> *"We make a living by what we get,*
> *but we make a life by what we give. "*
>
> *- Sir Winston Churchill*

Goldrush Fever

During the 1880's, thousands of men lost their lives in an attempt to make it rich by prospecting gold. They trekked thousands of miles, enduring hardship, freezing temperatures and starvation while trying to obtain the prized commodity. They believed it would be their ticket to happiness and freedom. However, many of those who reaped the greatest profits from the goldrush were not the gold diggers, or those who panned for gold.

Some entrepreneurs saw a market in selling distilled spirits to 'uplift' the spirits of the despondent prospectors who found no gold. Other profiteers earned their bounty servicing before and after markets created by the goldrush. Those who saw opportunity in selling picks, shovels and axes took fewer risks, and were guaranteed a return for their efforts. Most often when we do something that we enjoy, we excel, and the financial gain will follow. Satisfaction comes from doing the right things for the right reasons.

Time out:

Why are you doing what you do for a career? Has your ingenuity enabled you to find a niche which fulfils both your financial needs and your need for job satisfaction?

Identity by Association

The alarm clock no longer lets out a shrill reminder that it is six o'clock. John doesn't sleepily smash the snooze button, so he can savor an extra ten minutes of sleep. Announcements about snarled rush hour traffic are of no relevance. The receptionist at the office doesn't await his morning reports about the drivers who cut him off, or his complaining about the endless rain. Meetings at the office go on without him in fact, few really notice or care that his chair was filled by someone else.

John retired last year. He isn't the CEO of the Fortune 500 company, nor is he the president of the Board of Trade. He handed in the card that admitted him to exclusive fitness facilities and dinner clubs. He is no longer Chairman of the Board of Directors for the Regional Planning Committee or Deputy Minister of the Department of Health and Social Development. It seemed only right that he also resign his positions as Vice President of the Business and Professional Club for his profession, and the two executive positions he held in local service clubs.

John is despondent - it seems like there is nothing, just a big void. John did not know himself, and he had no hobbies. His work had been his life. He had defined himself by his job and his affiliation with work related organizations. His success had been in part a result of the long hours he spent networking in the service clubs. Other people recognized him, not as John Davis, but as a CEO of a company or the president of a certain club. His sense of security came from his job, as did his status in the community. John Davis, as a person, seemed only to exist in theory.

John is not alone. Men and women who achieve status and security through their work, often face depression when it is suddenly taken away from them. They lack a sense of identity and depend only on the identity created through their association with organizations. They love the security - the sense of importance - the sense of identity it provides.

It is very important that these types of people receive support through the transition. They need to develop a passionate interest in other activities. Those who don't, are the ones who die sudden, premature deaths within a few years of retirement.

People who have done well in their careers are often the most at risk when lay-off or retirement occurs. Most often, high achievers are type A personalities. They require big challenges, are risk takers and need more stimulation than their peers. Passion is most important. They can be kept busy doing a number of different things, but unless it lights the fire of passion in their lives, they will not survive the transition.

Time out:
How well do you know yourself? What are the things that bring meaning to your life? How will you fulfil these values in a way that will bring value to your life beyond the realms of your job? Is your life balanced?

Changing the Employment Paradigm

The juice machine salesman was confident that his juicer removed every drop of juice from lemons. He offered $1,000 in cash to the first person who could squeeze any juice out of the lemon after his juice machine was finished with it. His offer was great for business, until a small man with sunken cheeks stepped forward. To everyone's amazement, he squeezed enough juice from the lemon to make three glasses of lemonade. "Amazing", commented the salesman, "but how did you do that?"

"Quite simple", responded the man, "I'm from the Income Tax Department." Like the salesman, we all succumb to the tax department. We may earn enough - we just don't get to keep enough. Most of us are working longer and harder for less than ever before.

Many of our beliefs regarding employment are socially determined. Work fulfils psychological, sociological, and economic needs in our lives. We judge jobs by the salary they produce. We frequently encourage teenagers to make career choices based only on salaries. Making career decisions based on income alone is a sure path to job dissatisfaction.

Jobs that allow the participant to make discretionary decisions, while allowing independence, are more likely to provide psychological satisfaction. Although obesity, diet and smoking are considered to be risk factors for heart attacks, half the people who have heart attacks have none of these risk factors. However, almost all heart attack patients are victims of job dissatisfaction.

Suppose a man says, "I would love to own a Bed and Breakfast business when I retire. My present job is secure, but I hate it. However, if I stick it out, I will have a good retirement package". Waiting for retirement would provide the financial security of a pension to back him up, as he establishes the business. It may seem quite logical, but is his decision to stay in a job he hates a good decision?

Although he may really believe that he is in control of his future, his actions do not demonstrate this. He expresses other beliefs that mask or distort his ability to accomplish his real dream. He may be afraid of what people would think if he quit a secure job to start a Bed and Breakfast. The *fear of what others may think* can create a barrier to change.

Precisely who are these people who are so important that their opinion is more important than his own? Maybe they are not specific individuals. Strive to find the career path and lifestyle that will bring you satisfaction. You will never satisfy society.

Many people have bought into a societal norm that is as old as the Industrial Revolution which suggests all except the very wealthy must be wage earners. Statistics indicate that between 1976 and 1994, the number of self-employed people doubled. Entrepreneurial skills are becoming necessary for survival in our changing economy.

Society may, from a great distance, seem homogeneous. But things are often not the way they appear. Within any society there are almost as many opinions as there are people. For every person who thinks this man should keep his job, there will be just as many who would tell him to do something else.

One person will perceive farming as the best opportunity for this person. Another will try to sell him on being a truck driver. Another will say he should get more formal education. Someone will try to convince him he will make his *million* by joining the latest network marketing opportunity. The list may go on and on, with as many solutions as there are people consulted.

Very few people in the society he so reveres, even care what he does. Most people don't even know his name. Those who do aren't really concerned about his financial decisions or life style. In fact, if he were to die tomorrow - a few people would show up to a service honoring his life. The majority would then leave, and in a very short time forget all about him.

We become like marionettes on a set of strings, moving this way and that, trying to provide appearances that will appease the crowd. Often the crowd is not even observing, and we still practice our routine.

We date the "approved" date, we marry for reasons we believe matter in our society. We strive to become the *typical* family, with adequate finances to have two cars, and a sprawling bungalow on a view lot with a swimming pool. We add to that a boat, or motorhome, and countless other objects we perceive as symbols of status and worth. We buy objects we can't afford, to impress people we don't even like, and they don't even take notice.

Trying to hide the fact that we are not as happy as we ought to be, our actions reinforce the reality we have bought into. We rush to the overcrowded bus, or jostle for a place in rush hour traffic so we can race home to another meal of packaged food, eaten in front of the television. We watch catchy ads that reinforce our food choices. Thoughtless and mesmerized, we watch as actors who are paid big dollars, portray the lifestyle we are living.

This provides confirmation that our lives are perfectly normal by the sitcom standard, or better than normal compared to the soaps. Boredom sets in, and in our efforts to find a panacea, we surf the talk shows. Our life is never so bazaar that we can't find someone who is more dysfunctional than we are somewhere on the tube.

Television now has a rival. Surfing the Internet, is the latest craze. Some people spend four to six hours daily on the Internet. Any leisure activity which consumes that much time is robbing you of other opportunities. Allowing one activity to take up all your time results in a lack of balance, and diminishes your availability for other opportunities.

Television watching and Internet surfing can separate us from a meaningful reality. Family communication stops, and other interests are neglected. We bury our true self deeper and ignore our intuitions which tell us there is more to life than this. And the cycle continues.

We all know of families where this cycle leads to the total destruction of the family unit. These individuals become increasingly dysfunctional as they try even harder to bury their pain. Just around the corner there is a family like this. The wife has become an alcoholic in her attempt to escape her pain. The husband has become a workaholic. Their children, crying for attention, have become dependent on marijuana, then other street drugs combined with alcohol. This cycle often starts because they have adopted the belief that objects and money bring happiness.

Objects do not bring happiness, and are not a measurement of success. Success comes from the process of honoring the inner self. The self we by nature should be allowing to grow, develop, and blossom.

Living in this mode keeps one so busy that there is no time to awaken to the higher sense of who we are. We become too preoccupied to meditate. We cannot find time to be in tune with ourselves and nature. We cling to what is familiar and stay locked in our comfort zone. The powerful influence of doing something for long enough, is that after a while we adopt it as our reality. All new information is jaded as we channel it through the fallacies which have replaced our core beliefs and values.

Adopting dysfunctional life styles leads to rejecting change, and choosing to remain in our *comfort* zone. All too often, we aren't in a comfort zone at all. It is a *discomfort* zone!

Therefore, the more often and deeper we are willing to dig into our beliefs, the more clearly we will understand what we do to sabotage our own successes. Superficial self-examination leads to superficial change. The best solution is to get to know yourself and determine what you need to make your dreams a reality. Explore why you really do what you are doing. Give some thought to the psychological needs that are fulfilled through work.

From the time we are born, the stimuli around us affects our development and either meets or deprives us of our psychological needs. From the day we become a member of a family, our lives are being shaped. As we mature into young adults, we start to make decisions more frequently on our own. At this stage, we consider the opinions of our parents as less and less important - in some cases, young adults rebel against the beliefs of their parents.

Individuation, or the process of becoming separated from parents, is part of the natural course of development and necessary for us to reach a state of independence. Too often we see ourselves as independent, yet we are still trying to achieve goals that belong to others.

As our adult life continues, our choices bring continual changes in our lives. The most important lesson for us to learn is that we must follow our own path. Achieving career goals that are psychologically satisfying is one of the most important aspects of our careers.

Time out:
What does being successful mean to you? What do you wish to achieve, other than financial security, from your career?

Creativity and Productivity

Adulthood is the stage of life when we contribute to the productivity or creativity of our generation. Adults provide for the physical and financial needs of the next generation. Most adults procreate and nurture children. By nurturing children, we assist in shaping the very ones who will become the decision makers of the future.

Adults can choose not to contribute to society, doing only the minimum necessary to get by - becoming dependent on social systems for even the basic needs of life. If this is their choice, they become stagnant. Society needs safety nets for short term intervention. However, continuous dependence on social intervention creates *colonies of parasites*, who have no intention of becoming contributors. People who operate using this paradigm always want more - for doing less. Giving them more only creates greater dependency.

Stagnation occurs when the individual lacks concern for society or future generations. Stagnation results in being self-absorbed and bored with life. Eventually, this leads to a sense of emptiness and a nagging sense of loss. They may come to the *golden years* of life and instead of being filled with a feeling of accomplishment, they are filled with disappointment and despair. There are many old people in nursing homes, who are there only because they have given up.

As adults, we instinctively seek to find a meaning for our lives. Experiences such as divorce, or the unexpected death of a close friend, trigger the reflection process. Reflection often happens when we reach forty or fifty years of age, and again at or after retirement.

Adults in their senior years need to be able to reflect on their lives and feel they have made a meaningful contribution to society. Seniors who accept themselves as they are, have a sense of satisfaction from their efforts and choices. Those who are satisfied with their lives, may feel that they acquired the kind of wisdom which comes only with age.

Conversely, those who feel they have not accomplished much in life, feel disappointed. They feel frustrated, cheated, that they have been victimized or disenfranchised by the system. They are filled with regret. They live in fear of death, and wish they could live their lives over again.

It is very sad to see people suffering emotionally because of regrets from the past. The only thing that could be sadder than seeing others reach that state, is to reach that state ourselves. The best insurance against spending our senior years filled with regret, is to live every day to its fullest. Make life happen while age is on your side, then later in life there will be fewer regrets.

I think we should all stop referring to our careers as work. Work is defined as *the effort of doing or making something, or a factory or place for doing or making something.* The definition of job is even more depressing. Job is defined as *something a person has to do.* The problem with this definition is the word *has* -something a person *has* to do. It isn't a choice, much less a passion. We really need to change our paradigms regarding our creative endeavors.

How different it would be if we looked at each day as an *opportunity to create!* Instead of saying, "I have a job at the office of Bjornsen, Bell, Beiderweiden, Bennet and Belfontaine", - say "I have an opportunity to create, at the Law Office of Bjornsen, Bell, Beiderweiden, Bennet and Belfontaine". Or if you can't handle that, say "I have an opportunity to produce at the Law Office of Bjornsen, Bell, Beiderweiden, Bennet and Belfontaine". The concept of it being a job - *something someone has to do,* is gone - the sense of drudgery is gone. Change it to *opportunity* and what a difference it makes to the level of passion. It is now much better than a job!

To be psychologically healthy in old age, we must create and produce in our younger years. The word *productive* comes from the root word *to produce.* When we produce we *cause something to be,* that would not have been there otherwise. I like the word *create* even better. The definition of create is *to make a thing that has not existed before; to make something original by intelligence and skill; to give rise to, or to cause.* Isn't every interaction with other people, whether you are a grocery store clerk or university professor, a creation of something original? Every conversation, service, or product we produce has an identity, and is new - therefore it is our creation.

The whole concept of employ and employment is equally as fraught with negative connotations. The dictionary says employ means *use the services of; give work.* If you are being *used by* someone, does it feel good? Not likely, and if they use you for work or a job it is even more depressing! Employment is defined as *what a person does for a living; work.* There is no sense of fulfilment in that. Your life in exchange for a few coins. Sounds like a prison sentence to me!

Are you looking for an *opportunity to create* or an *opportunity to produce?* Or are you presently in an *opportunity to create* or an *opportunity to produce?* Simply changing the terminology will not change the attitude or behavior. We must change the beliefs we have regarding work. Thinking from this new paradigm will make a big difference.

If changing the terminology sounds a little crazy, think of when we adopted the terms *Ms.* and *letter carrier.* Those sounded weird too. Some words, once commonly used are now grounds for disciplinary action in the corporate setting. Imagine what would happen to an office manager if he used sexist terms to refer to his typist. Yet thirty years ago sexist language was used frequently in some offices.

Although sexism is less prevalent in the workplace, changing the terminology has made little difference to the few who persist in offending. This is because these individuals have changed part of their behavior without making any changes to their beliefs. However, changing the semantics has increased awareness and most individuals believe in the merit of the changes and act accordingly.

If we change the paradigm first, then the new words will seem more appropriate, and we will have no problem changing the semantics. Try it! It is just one little step - not too much - risk, and imagine the difference it could make.

The best insurance against despair, at any age in life, is to:

- Take control.
  Accomplish things that hold meaning to you.
- Become a master of change.
  Understanding the process of change enables you
  to become skillful in initiating change.
- Stop working.
  Start creating or producing. "Up your job" - you
  are in an "opportunity to create."

Career Transition

> *"Liberty means responsibility. That is why most men dread it."*
>
> *- George Bernard Shaw*

Having an education and/or set of skills is not everything. Without a market you are still unemployed. Self employment can be a solution for some people, however, it is not a panacea. Joining the *self-unemployed,* who believe they are self-employed and have never made a sale is not the answer. Nor is becoming a part of the *self-under-employed* who delude themselves into thinking they will make it someday.

Deciding to start a home based business and getting a business phone installed, doesn't mean you are in business. If the only time the phone rings is when you use your residential line to phone the business line just so you can hear your business phone ring - that is a problem. If you have so much spare time that you call your business phone number ten times a day, it is time to get help - and I don't mean hiring someone to help you operate the business!

You must find a way to make the connection between your skills and/or education, and those who have the purchasing power and authority to buy. The first step is to identify the product or service you can (and want to) provide. Remember that it must fulfil more than your financial needs. It must be something that will be valued and wanted by others. Whether we are looking for a new job, a new career, or deciding to pursue self-employment, the steps in the process are similar.

Identifying Skills and Experience

There is an important fundamental difference between skills and experience. Experience is what you did, whereas skills are how you did it. Listing where you worked, your job title, and your duties is usually the best way to determine your experience.

Using active words to describe your work experience is a skill that is valuable for writing your resume. Most good resume writing books provide excellent lists of active and descriptive words. Consult your local bookstore or library to find these resources. The purpose of our discussion for this book is to clarify the role of experience and skills in the decision making process.

It is most helpful to determine all your experience gained through duties performed at past jobs, volunteer work, and personal interests. Then, after you have worked through the rest of the process, return to clarify and emphasize the experience and skills that will be most beneficial to your future path.

Some people find it more difficult to list their skills than their experience. To sell your services to a prospective employer, you need to be able to articulate *how* those duties assisted you in learning transferable skills. This is also very necessary if you are pursuing self-employment.

Some skills are directly related to the duty performed. For instance, if you have been a hamburger flipper for Fiona's Fast Foods, your obvious skills are determining the timing and order of preparation to make the perfect burger. Your experience includes the ability to follow orders established by the supervisor or company. This is a transferable skill. However, knowing how to make a burger will do little to get you away from the grill, into a position as a day camp co-ordinator (supposing that is your chosen path).

The skills that are implicit in the hamburger flipper example are: the ability to work as an efficient team member; remain organized; work well under pressure; communicate effectively with other staff members and the public. These skills are the real marketable part of your work experience. In developing an understanding of your skills, you can perhaps separate the aspects of the job you liked from the parts you did not like. It wasn't necessary to like flipping those burgers for you to enjoy the team atmosphere. Identifying the aspects you enjoyed, enables you to become more focussed on the options that lay open to you for your future.

Time out:
List your skills and experience. Remember to include skills and experience acquired through volunteer work and hobbies.

Identifying your Interests

Identifying your interests based on the things you liked and disliked from your previous experiences is the first step in planning your career path. Some people find their interests are very diversified. Others find they have few interests. To further clarify your interests, it is beneficial to examine your personal values.

Understanding your inner self and your core beliefs is crucial to this process. This requires deep introspection and self-examination. It requires separating the beliefs you have adopted from your family, society and your peers. It requires a willingness to question and define the meaning of your life. Developing Purpose and Mission Statements is an excellent part of this process. Once you understand your purpose in life you have much less difficulty explaining what interests you and why. You are clearer about who you are and what you want to accomplish in life. Interests then are those things we enjoy and appreciate, based on beliefs we hold about ourselves and the universe.

Exploring your interests from this perspective enables you to become more in tune with your inner self. It takes far less effort to make meaningful career decisions if you are grounded and centered. This will answer to your spirituality - regardless how you perceive your personal spirituality. It leads to a sense of congruence and enables you to do the right things for the right reasons.

When our self-actualization needs are filled we have a sense of satisfaction with life. It filters down to fill lower level psychological needs. Financial needs are met automatically, because you are beginning at the top of Maslow's hierarchy of needs.

From this perspective, the issues are not important. The vision is fulfilment of your personal mission and purpose. The income you earn becomes a by-product of the vision. It reverses how you perceive economic downturns and your place in the work force.

Time out:

What are your interests? Do your interests and careers have a commonality? Can a career transition bring you closer to your interests?

Lifestyle Considerations

Examining your personal values may clarify that you enjoy the quieter lifestyle of a rural setting. Likely you will not be able to live in the country, if you choose a career that requires you to work in the center of a big metropolis. Commuting a great distance in heavy traffic would contradict the goal of enjoying a slower paced lifestyle. Yet year after year, hundreds of people move farther and farther out of the metropolis to achieve a slower lifestyle.

Tens of thousands of people commute long distances to work every day. For example, a university professor was already living a one hour commute from work. He and his wife decided to move out to more open spaces and a quieter lifestyle to raise their young sons. Subsequently, he changed jobs and added another hour to the commute. Now he spends two hours morning and evening, battling rush hour traffic.

This man assumes he is putting his family first. Although he thinks he is doing what is best for his young sons, his thinking is flawed. When we as individuals, neglect to do what is best for ourselves, the consequences are never better for the lives of the other members of our family. A man who has spent four hours commuting, and eight hours working, has no time to be a husband and a father.

Even if he contends that the drive allows him time to unwind from the pressures of the job - it still is a drain of energy, and driving in rush hour traffic is undeniably stressful, even for the most relaxed drivers.

Therefore, deciding where you want to work is not enough. Career planning must not

> *"A child is like the inexperienced birdwatcher for whom every bird is a first. The adult is the experienced veteran who approaches each sighting with a highly complicated set of expectations and a great deal of experience against which to check what he sees; every field identification for him is structured by these past experiences."*
>
> *- Harry L. Miller*

overlook lifestyle. Your career consumes approximately one third of your day-time hours, so the lifestyle your creativity or productivity (work) brings to you is a crucial part of your overall satisfaction.

Time out:

Have you considered the impact your chosen career will have on your family life? How does it affect your proximity and availability to participate in leisure activities you enjoy? Do you prefer to work indoors or outdoors; with things or people; with your hands or your mind?

The Role of Education

Education can open our eyes to see new horizons for ourselves, and can provide us with adequate information to make self-directed changes. Unfortunately for some, education merely becomes another experience used to reinforce reality "as it is," instead of a tool for exploring the reality that "could be." Therefore, optimum education, which includes critical and creative thinking skills, is important whether we are self-employed, working for an employer, changing careers, or continuing on the same path.

Education includes formal and informal learning. Many adults pursue self-directed learning outside formal educational institutions. This is great, and is becoming increasingly accepted as valid for obtaining credentials. Colleges and universities are becoming more open to providing credit toward accredited programs for work experience, and for independent and/or self-directed study. This is usually referred to as PLA (Prior Learning Assessment).

If you believe you have significant knowledge and experience in a particular field, it may be well worth checking the PLA requirements of several colleges and universities. Credentials are quick, easy ways for prospective employers to assess your skills and knowledge, and should not be overlooked.

Education, whether formal or informal, provides knowledge and skills, however, it also provides psychological needs. Education leads to personal growth, and a clearer understanding of the world around us. It is an invaluable tool for achieving satisfaction from life.

Additional education opportunities are becoming more available through advances in technology. Interactive, information-oriented, computer-assisted education is becoming available through access to the Internet. I have completed one university course in this manner. It is the leading edge of distance education for the twenty-first century. Similarly, satellite and CD Rom bring people and knowledge together in new ways.

When you stop learning, you stop living. In university lectures forty, sixty, and eighty year olds take their seats along side the nineteen year olds. Formal and informal learning opportunities are not restricted by youth or old age. In itself, acquiring new skills and knowledge is a fulfilling activity at any age. Life-long learning enables you to grow and develop and is a necessary part of self-actualization.

Time out:

What is your educational plan? Do you intend to participate in formal education? Do you make an effort to learn something new every day?

Entrepreneurship: Is it for you?

People who are self-employed must learn to deal with fluctuations in their income. At times it may mean that your living expenses exceed your profit for the month. Some first time entrepreneurs are like the young sales associate who misunderstood her boss' talk on perseverance. The boss stated "If you persevere in seeing enough potential clients, the law of averages will pay you $143.50 for every call." The young sales associate was filled with enthusiasm and went immediately to her grandfather. He had no use for the product she was selling, so he declined. "Thanks, grandpa," the young sales associate replied, "that's okay. I just made $143.50." The grandfather informed her he did not quite understand, but if that was how she earned her money, he would let her come again anytime!

If you want to be your own boss, you either need to have a lot of business sense or you need to hire a consultant. The consultant can assist you until you have time to learn some of the basic skills of operating a business.

A self-employed individual needs to be able to wear many different hats. Let's discuss the traits that motivate individuals to pursue entrepreneurial ventures.

An entrepreneur must be driven by passion toward a clearly articulated vision. He or she often sees opportunities where others think none exist. (Unfortunately, sometimes the others are right!) If the entrepreneur sets up shop and later finds strong competitors open one on each side, he or she doesn't give up. When one of them puts up a sign saying "Best Prices," and the other puts up a sign, "Outstanding Service," he or she sees the opportunity and hangs a sign that says "Main Entrance."

Motivational factors for entrepreneurs may include all or some of the following desires, beliefs and/or values:

- Monetary gains are directly linked to personal efforts, therefore the belief that there is a possibility of making more money than in a corporate structure.
- Desire to pursue a personal and professional challenge which enables more creativity and self-directed management.
- To prove to self and/or others you can do it. (Personally, I would ask some questions to challenge this perspective - based on our earlier discussion about attempting to impress society).
- Increased opportunity for personal and professional growth.
- Independence and ability to choose hours of business. (This can also be a slippery slope. Will you, or will your clients determine your hours?)
- Personal vision and purpose. Belief in the ability to make a difference, or to provide a superior product or service.

What qualities do you need to identify in yourself, BEFORE you choose to become your own boss? Successful entrepreneurs usually share most of the following characteristics:

- Like people and have excellent interpersonal skills
- Have good leadership qualities
- Good decision makers
- Understand the importance of having a written plan
- Have good health, high energy and drive
- Enjoy independence
- Self-disciplined
- Establish priorities and follow through
- Demonstrate determination - do not give up easily
- Can be creative enough to adapt quickly to change
- Have a good level of self-confidence

- Have always enjoyed being achievers
- Hard workers
- Well organized
- Enjoy research and use it to keep up to date
- Optimistic
- Tend to enjoy risks
- Assume responsibility through own initiative
- Have excellent knowledge and skill level in chosen field

Interestingly, people who identify what they really love to do and choose to do it, often find they work more hours - not so much out of necessity - but because they love their work!

Time out:

Would you like a boss who is just like you? Could that boss be you? Do you have the characteristics which would enable you to be successful if you were in business for yourself?

Organizational Structures

From a sociological point of view, the workplace is an institution - (not the building, but the organization of the company). The organizational structure may become our personal prison if it is incompatible with our personal needs. Conversely, it may meet our social needs if it is a good fit. Socially, the workplace provides a sense of identity and belonging; an avenue to relate to peers; an opportunity to fulfil our need for creativity and productivity. The structure of the organization includes: the designation of authority; the operational policies and procedures; job design; formal systems for control.

Bureaucratic structures often provide little room for individuals to make decisions. The hierarchy and responsibilities of the organization are defined. Sometimes, people at the lower end of the hierarchy work very hard, only for a superior to get all the credit.

The individual employee is bound by rules, having little authority to enact changes. In large bureaucracies, decisions are made from the top down, or when steering committee members reach a consensus. Protocol must be adhered to at all times. In politically based bureaucracies, the mandate may shift, along with shifts in power.

The leadership in corporations becomes more decentralized when regional or branch managers are allowed to make decisions. Decentralized leadership is consistent with McGregor's (1960)[1] "Theory Y", suggesting that individual workers are intrinsically self motivated. They do not need to be closely supervised in order to get the job done. Responsibilities shift and change as necessary.

Management may be autocratic, democratic or laissez-faire. Each management style alters the structure of the institution. The autocratic manager is more regimented and less flexible in what he or she sees as the way to get the job done. The democratic manager considers the opinion of the employees, and allows more room for individuals to design their own way to get the work done. The laissez-faire leadership style is the most open and flexible. It is more of a teamwork atmosphere where discretionary decision making is equally shared by all participants in the environment.

The flatter model of management is becoming more the norm as middle management positions fall prey to the scalpel of corporate downsizing. In this style of management, interdependence and cooperation are important. Managers and workers share skills and decision making responsibilities. More teamwork is expected between employees. It is more important than ever to take individual responsibility for productivity. When working in an organization, our destiny is often dependent upon our contribution to the corporate goals.

The 1990's brought rapid technical advances. Both the self-employed and those employed in the corporate sector need to educate themselves constantly to stay current with the new technology and

---

McGregor, D. (1960) The Human Side of Enterprise. New York: McGraw Hill.

information. We either adapt, or become outdated. Adopting a lifelong learning perspective helps ensure that we will not be swept out of the work force because of the inability to adapt to changing times.

Corporate downsizing, economic downturns, takeovers, mergers and divestures, continue to occur and threaten job stability. It is no longer a reality to start a career, rise through the ranks, and retire. Golden handshakes are becoming more common than golden watches. One appeal of self-employment is the greater sense of control over one's career. Statisticians frequently tell us that the likelihood of a business failing in the first five years is very high. The part they do not address in the same statistical report, is this: Of those who are working - how many will be employed in the same job in five years?

Mid-life seems to be the time when stagnation and burn out are most likely to occur. Countless people approach their forties and find all kinds of unexpected events starting to happen. We either initiate change, or fall victim to the changes that come when we fail to plan. This could be aptly called the "Shift Happens" stage of life.

For many people in this age bracket there is a sense that they are no longer in control of their lives. The chaos may be started by unexpected divorce, or an aging parent becoming their dependent, or their empty nest refilling with adult children and rambunctious young grandchildren. It escalates. There is the adoption of the neighborhood stray cat...the take over of the corvette payments - even though you won't be the one driving it...and the acquisition of a seven foot rubber tree that outgrew your friend's apartment...the roof begins to leak...the hot water tank needs replacing...your dog becomes aggressive (jealous of the adopted cat)...the green space beside your home is rezoned for high density residential development...layoff occurs resulting in a big change to your pension...your sister gets ill and so on goes the list of things that bring chaos to your already out of control life.

We assume responsibility for keeping everyone else happy... forgetting our responsibility for our own happiness. We say we are just being conscientious...the reality is, too often we get cold feet when we need to stick up for ourselves. When these things occur, some people find themselves emotionally, physically, and financially bankrupt.

My research has shown that many baby boomers are boomed out. They have financed themselves to the hilt, and bottomed out because the things in which they placed their confidence have failed them. Their marriage, career, or finances and possessions have failed to bring them satisfaction. Viewing our lives in a more holistic sense can be helpful at all ages. Our lives can be compartmentalized into work, social, family, financial, physical and leisure. However, all areas impact all other areas.

Perhaps job tenure and permanency are not as great as they appear. Stagnation can easily occur for people who stay in one position with one company for a very long time. I recently saw several examples of this while attending university. In particular, two professors who had been in the same department at the same institution, had become very stagnant and burned out. Students who had taken courses fifteen or seventeen years earlier from the same professors, found their enthusiasm and inspiration had been replaced with bitterness, cynicism and boredom.

Without continually learning, we can become obsolete. However, if we do not broaden our horizons, we can also become over-specialized. Over-specialization can make us less useful to the corporation, and can be dastardly if we find ourselves out pounding the pavement for new opportunity. It is healthy to develop a secondary interest, and not rely totally on only one field of expertise.

Lifelong learning also prevents our tendency to reach a point of being promoted to a level of incompetence. Each time we go for a promotion, we reach the top of our skills and abilities. If we do not continue to develop skills and knowledge, we become ineffective. As corporations strive to trim their budgets, corporate-sponsored training becomes less available and the responsibility falls on the individual.

During retirement, you are your own boss. If you have not learned the skills necessary to bring meaning to your life without the leadership of an employer, by the time you reach this stage, it could be a difficult transition. A sense of purpose during retirement is equally as important as during our working life.

Fulfilment in our senior years may come from volunteer work, or participation in special interest groups, or creative ventures. Activities such as writing, arts, or crafts can contribute to a meaningful retirement. Retirees who enjoy the business world can choose to become mentors to younger people. It keeps seniors mentally alert, and provides them with a sense of self-worth. It also benefits the younger generation, and is a great way to celebrate the contributions of the older generation.

Time out:

Does the structure of the organization where you work support your needs? Do you have a mentor, or are you a mentor? Are you allowing the needs of others to create chaos in your life? How are you taking care of your own needs?

Select-a-Boss

Most people look for a job with the attitude that they want someone to hire them. This premise is, whether we realize it or not, buying into the belief that someone else - not yourself - has control of your destiny. Looking for an "opportunity to create" with an enabler or enabling firm would be a much better idea.

Unfortunately, many people who are seeking jobs - don't really want to work. A young woman had made an appointment with a CEO with the hope of getting a job. The CEO informed her that his company was already overstaffed, and that there wasn't enough work for the

> *"We are all functioning at a small fraction of our capacity to live fully in its total meaning of loving, caring, creating and adventuring. Consequently, the actualizing of our potential can become the most exciting adventure of our lifetime."*
>
> *- Herbert Otto*

existing staff. "Sounds just like the kind of place I would like to work," she volunteered, "I do so little work, no one will even notice if you hire me." It is just amazing what people say in interviews!

Next time you think a job interview is difficult, try to imagine it from the other side of the desk - there you are, the prospective employer, trying to assess whether you are willing to pay thousands of dollars to train this total stranger. You have to make a decision based on a twenty minute interview. You may spend more time in a week with this person than you do with the spouse it took you three years to make up your mind about.

A politician who lost an election, was forced to look for work. He insisted that he could do the job better than anyone else, and within a month or two, profits of the business would double. He assured the interviewer that dozens of major corporations were vying for contracts with him.

"That's impressive", said the manager. "Now what are your weak points?"

"There is only one, sir", the politician-wanna-be stated, "I have been known to exaggerate frequently."

We all have weak points, and the prospective employer wants to know what we intend to do about them. Maybe you are disorganized.

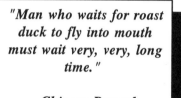

"Man who waits for roast duck to fly into mouth must wait very, very, long time."

- Chinese Proverb

If you can say, "I recently attended a workshop on becoming more organized, and have been practicing the techniques presented," your willingness to address your problems will impress the interviewer. Sometimes it isn't what you admit on the job interview that counts most - it can be what you are unwilling to admit that may alert the prospective employer to your past performance. Evading questions or responding ambiguously immediately raises suspicions.

The dynamics of a job interview are affected by the meaning we give to work. If money and getting hired are all that matter, you will commit to the job without questioning if it is a suitable placement for you. Satisfied employees require less motivating, and bring a healthy attitude to work. If you don't want to be there - except on paydays - it is likely your supervisor won't want you there either.

The erroneous viewpoint, adopted by many, is that work should not be fun. If you are having fun, you must not be producing enough, or so seems the message in some workplaces. The workers accept the message, and the cycle continues. Although employment standards legislation clarifies terms and conditions for overtime, some employers seem to have various ways of assigning more than reasonable amounts of overtime. In times of higher unemployment, the fact that employees may fear leaving the job, is used to great advantage by this type of employer.

Sometimes, this shows up when the interviewer asks questions regarding your attitude to overtime, or hides the question discretely when asking about your commitment to your career. Employers who have devious ways of finding out a prospective employee's attitude, may be doing so in hopes of finding someone who will support his or her personal biases. No matter how badly you need an income, you should question the validity of working for this kind of employer.

So - what do you really want in a supervisor? You should do considerable research before going for an interview. A wealth of information can be gathered by networking. Finding other companies who do business with the company, or people who know people who work for the employer, can better equip you for the interview. The following questions may provide some things to consider:

- Is the employer reasonable when dealing with illness or other circumstances?
- Is the supervisor an effective communicator?
- Does the supervisor express appreciation or give credit for a job well-done?
- Do the supervisor and staff have positive attitudes?
- What is the morale within the company or department?
- Does the supervisor have effective leadership skills?
- Does the supervisor have a sense of humor?
- Does the employer promote from within the company?

It is important for you to find fulfilment in your work. This can only occur when there is a good match between the culture of the place of employment and the employee. Stop looking for an employer who can offer you a job, and start looking for an enabler who will provide you with an environment where you can have the best "opportunity to create" or "opportunity to produce." When you consider self-employment, you become your own enabler and you create your own "opportunity to create or produce".

Time out:
What should your employer be like? Do you want a supervisor who will allow you to have an active role in creating your work environment? Do you want to work in a team atmosphere, where your contributions are recognized for their worth, not by your rank in the hierarchy?

Designing a Career Plan

This is the last phase in the process of a job search or a career transition. Like education, this is a lifelong activity. It is becoming increasingly understood that the difference between mediocrity and excellence, or achieving success - is having a written plan.

The written plan provides a tool for measuring progress and for keeping your vision and purpose foremost at all times. When you have taken

> *"If you plan for a year, sow a seed.*
> *If you plan for a decade, plant a tree.*
> *If you plan for a century,*
> *educate the people."*
>
> *- Kuan-tzu*

the time to articulate your vision and your mission, you can immediately identify activities which will bring you closer to your goals.

We can have a lengthy list of goals, yet we will never accomplish them unless they are congruent with our personal beliefs and values. Taking the time to write our intentions and aspirations out, moves them from the subconscious to the conscious. This provides a clearer focus. Responding to situations and circumstances according to our Action Plan can enable us to create our ideal reality. Living without a written plan is like going canoeing without paddles. You may have a definite destination. However, it is unlikely you would ever reach it.

Care must be taken to ensure that your Action Plan is not a recipe for busywork. It can give the illusion that you are in control. If the reality is that you are involved in projects which provide the illusion of progress, without actual progress, you are just spinning your tires, and you are still stuck.

Busywork consumes energy. It is like chasing goats in a field without fences. When I was twelve, I was babysitting my two brothers, who were six and eight. A total stranger came to the door, and asked if we had seen any stray goats. He had bought two goats at an auction a mile away, and they had escaped while he was trying to load them.

I told him I hadn't seen the goats, but that I would be glad to help him find them. I decided my youngest brother wouldn't be able to run fast enough, so he should stay home, alone. Then my other brother and I went with the stranger, and spent two hours chasing through wheat fields, attempting to catch the goats. Numerous times we would spot them, but by the time we reached the place where we had seen the goats, they were long gone. I thought it was a great way to spend a warm summer afternoon. It was busywork!

Not only was it busywork for me, it created a crisis for my mother, and showed my irresponsibility in leaving my youngest brother. My mother's perception of the situation was much different than mine, or the stranger's! Take a look at your situation from someone else's perspective. How do they see it?

Time out:

Do the choices you make cause others undue stress and cause them to have to put out fires all the time? Are the decisions you make responsible? Are your decisions just an attempt to keep yourself so busy that you can ignore other things in your life that need to be dealt with?

Opportunity to Create a Difference

Central to job satisfaction is the sense that we are able to "make a difference." The need to make a difference is not restricted to people who choose careers which directly address human social needs - like psychologists, social workers or health care professionals. The difference we make may fit into a wide variety of descriptions, each one valid to the individual who pursues it.

The engineer who has a goal of developing robotics, sees herself or himself as improving working conditions for assembly line workers, and as providing a faster, more efficient way of manufacturing, so the end user can enjoy affordable products. The agriculturist sees value in improving food quality

> *What is Success?*
>
> *To laugh often and much;*
> *to win the respect of intelligent people and affection of children;*
> *to earn the appreciation of honest critics;*
> *to endure the betrayal of false friends;*
> *to appreciate beauty;*
> *to find the best in others;*
> *to leave the world a bit better, whether by a healthy child, a garden patch or a redeemed social condition;*
> *to know even only one life has breathed easier because you have lived.*
> *This is to have succeeded.*
>
> *- Ralph Waldo Emerson*

and the production as rewarding, because of the difference it makes to the lives of consumers and producers.

In reality, we are all serving the rest of humanity. The individual needs to pursue a career partly based on a belief that he or she has a contribution to make in the particular field being pursued.

Believing that our contribution is of value, changes our thinking from "I need this job," to "this job needs me." Doing things we truly believe in increases our commitment, and strengthens our desire to do the best possible job. Work done for the right reasons becomes pleasure, work done solely because we have to keep the debt collectors a few feet away from our door - is drudgery.

20/20 Vision: A Clear Focus

Each individual needs a clear focus. A clearly articulated vision statement needs to be neither too narrow, nor too broad. A narrow focus results in a limited reality. A focus that is too broad can be very similar to having no plan at all. Observe the following examples:

<u>The Narrow Focus</u>

I know what
I want. I want
to work for
the city of
Yourberg.
I want a job
that has no
overtime, no
irregular hours
- just 9 to 5
Mon. to Fri.
I want to
work in the
Taxation

Department
as a receptionist.
I want
Mary Doe
for a
Supervisor.

"Get serious"
you say!
"People don't
really do that."
And ... Yes
they do.
But if it
is only a
dream, not
a realistic
action plan
it will never
be a reality.
It will
become
an obstacle
instead of
a tool
for success.
Tina did
just that.
She met a
person who
encouraged
her to
believe the
difference
between
mediocre

accomplishments
and excellence
was getting a
BIG dream
and allowing
nothing and
nobody to
stand in
the way.

It was a
chance to
work with
celebrities
on the
big screen.
This person
was 'just' the
connection
she needed
to make
it happen.

After spending
hundreds of
hours doing
volunteer
work, (which
they praised
her for
immensely)
it became
obvious she
was not one
bit closer to
achieving the

dream. She
lacked certain
qualifications.
But she
thought
it was
time to
push for
a contract.
Yes, you
guessed it,
they would
have let her
volunteer
forever
- as for there
being any
opportunity
beyond that
it was not
there, never
was, never
would be.

Just trying
to read
something
that is
printed
like this is
difficult.
Imagine
living
your life
like this!

The Broad Focus

I just
want a job,
any job. My
car is near to being
repossessed. I have
lots of skills. I will work
long hours, for any company, even
for a miserable boss. I just want a job.
I have lots of skills, and I will read the job
ads from end to end and apply for every job I can.
(This approach is the "all over the place approach.")
This can't hurt, "it's a numbers game, isn't it" I rationalize.
In fact, I won't just look locally, I'd move if I got a job. I can
sell; or work with people; do office work; do cleaning; drive truck;
work on a production line; be a photographer; or a
waiter; or be a landscaper for the summer. There are
so many things I could do. I just want someone to
hire me, need a pay check. I don't even care
about wages or location. If it is a temporary
job, that is fine for now. In the midst of the
chaos I created, I suddenly realized - this is
just as dangerous as having too narrow a
focus. Answering every job would
require having several resumes
made up to target different
skills. The quality of my
responses to the ads
would be sacrificed. I would
not have the time to research the
company or to target my covering letters.
My covering letters would look like a computerized,

fill in the blanks bulk mail letter. More is not necessarily better.
Moreover, I cannot be all things to all people. There are some
jobs I am more suited to than others. No matter how
desperate I am, this is not the answer. There
are thousands of companies, and hundreds
of thousands of careers. I may get a
job this way, however it is
unlikely it would be long
term and I would soon
find myself out there
pounding the
streets...
AGAIN.
Soon my resume would look
like a patchwork quilt.

Time out:

*What are the skills you have already demonstrated? Are these
skills transferable to a different line of work? Do you wish to stay in
the type of career you have been in up until now, or do you feel it is
time for a change?*

*Have you determined which of your personal values influence
your definition of valuable work? What are the minimum and
maximum ranges of your present salary expectations? What are the
geographical boundaries of the area in which you wish to work?*

*Will you be employed or self-employed? How can you market
your skills? Do you want to use existing skills or get additional
training? What type of companies interest you? If you wish to be self-
employed, can you operate the business from your home? Will you
provide a product or service?*

*Are you doing something that has meaning to you? Are you
presently sacrificing your personal satisfaction and values, in an
environment that violates your needs for harmony and emotional
safety?*

Chapter 10

Beyond Mediocrity

> *"Health is a state of physical, mental and social well-being and is not merely the absence of disease and infirmity."*
>
> *- World Health Organization*

Well-being and Philosophy

Although this chapter is brief, that does not mean our physical well-being is less significant than other aspects of our lives. Physical health is an exhaustive topic, and cannot be completely addressed in this book. There are many available resources relating to fitness, nutrition, and relaxation. Therefore, we will discuss each of these areas only briefly, and discuss our physical well-being in a more philosophical sense.

Our North American health care system is under extreme stress, as the incidents of health related problems strain it to the limit. More people are looking to alternative medicine than ever before as they lose faith in the traditional medical system.

There are three philosophies we can choose to use as the foundation of our approach toward our physical well-being:

- Intervention and remedial care.
- Preventative health care.
- Optimum health and wellness.

Intervention and Remedial Health Care

The primary function of our medical health care system has traditionally been one of intervention and providing remedies. Government funded health care and insured health benefit programs, usually provide funding based on this philosophical outlook. Elective surgery may be only partially covered or not covered at all by insurance. This system pays to correct problems after they occur, and does little to invest in preventative care.

Treatments of this nature are usually invasive, and include surgery or drugs. While at times these methods are the only answer, it is far better to maintain our health. If we effectively maintain our health, we will seldom, if ever, have to resort to these types of treatments.

Although more effort is being made to educate people about the cause of disease, budgets for education are minimal compared to the money spent on fixing problems. From this perspective, the system becomes so involved in *putting out fires* that there are few resources left for *preventing the fires.*

Within this system, prevention springs from grassroots movements, more often than not. Recent movements to stop cigarette smoking come more from a grassroots level than from the medical community. While Stop Smoking campaigns have been effective, and directly address a recognized health risk, this is a very small part of a much larger problem. The public frequently is unaware of the steps they could be taking to prevent disease. Many times we learn the information only after someone in our family has been stricken with a disease.

Often we operate on only partial information. We may, for instance, know that we should eat a high fibre diet. What we may not know is how much fibre we need, or where we will find that amount of fibre. Influenced by advertising, we erroneously assume that *one* bowl of high fibre breakfast cereal is the answer to all of our daily fibre needs. We may not know, for example, that lack of fibre is linked to cancer of the colon.

Some medical doctors are more inclined than their colleagues, to promote a more preventative approach. Teaching prevention is time consuming. Frequently they do not have the time they need, with individual patients, to be able to do it as effectively as they would like.

The information is available. The problem is more often than not, an unrealistic dependency on doctors. Some people expect their doctor to provide them with all the information they need. The patient needs to take more responsibility. This may include reading, attending workshops, learning about nutrition and participating in physical activity.

An Ounce of Prevention

In addition to the medical doctors who are becoming more concerned with prevention, there are a host of alternative practitioners who focus on prevention. Many of these healing arts have been around for centuries. Most have faced, at times, stiff opposition from the medical community. However, increasing numbers of people are opting to choose alternatives to conventional medical care, and some medical doctors are becoming more open to the benefits of these therapies.

In part, a shift is only possible if individuals in the medical community become willing to look at the alternatives objectively. Unfortunately, the lucrative pharmaceutical industry often holds a powerful influence. Decisions may be based on finances rather than the well-being of the public.

The increased acceptance of alternatives comes from the increased level of education in our society. People are recognizing their right to get a second medical opinion and/or to explore other options.

Each year more people who face a dismal prognosis based on medical reports, are choosing to look for other sources of help. Many people believe that alternative therapies are at least as effective as the medical profession's methods of treatment, for life threatening diseases. While alternative therapies are not viewed by most people as the first resort in the treatment of serious ailments, increasing numbers of people are willing to explore alternative therapies. Many of these are pleasantly surprised by the results.

The alternative health care professions are not usually as closely aligned to intervention and remedial treatment philosophies that are widely accepted by government and/or private insurance programs. This means they usually rely on a user fee system. Even when the government or private insurance fund their services, the ceiling on expenditures is much more restricted than it is for medical treatment of the same condition. When the conservative approach to medical and alternative therapies is accepted, it is usually in conjunction with a preventative health care philosophy.

Prevention is at least one step toward accepting individual responsibility. Along with this, we also need to examine our beliefs regarding how we treat our bodies. All too often we live with an "it can't happen to me" attitude toward illness. Altering our health related habits is only possible if we have values and beliefs that support wellness.

Optimum Health and Wellness

Wellness is not merely the absence of symptoms. We can be very ill and not have any symptoms. Have you known anyone who appeared to be healthy, and died suddenly from heart disease, or who did not find out their body was full of cancer until it was too late?

The World Health Organization defines Health as "a state of physical, mental and social well-being and not merely the absence of disease and infirmity."

The word wellness is not in most dictionaries. The medical health care system, too often treats only symptoms, and ignores the need to enable us to achieve - not just absence of disease, but optimum health.

Extended stress and emotional distress can lead to stress related disease. Long before it gets that far, the anxiety caused by a dysfunctional lifestyle can manifest itself by severe pain in the solar plexus. We may feel like our heart is breaking, or we are forcing ourselves not to cry. We may find ourselves unable to sleep, or prone to overeating or occasionally unable to eat at all.

As individuals, and as a nation, we cannot be emotionally and mentally healthy if we operate from unhealthy paradigms. The qualities and skills which enable us to cope and to move beyond coping - to getting what we want to get out of life - are not learned by osmosis from our surroundings. We form habits based on repetition or social conditioning and respond accordingly. Changing these responses often requires a lot of hard work. Revitalizing our true potential is only possible when we remove the barriers caused by past conditions.

We must establish habits that set us free to reach our potential. Our bodies are intricate self monitoring organisms which are able to sustain our existence. However, the human body is capable of functioning at a higher level of efficiency, that moves us from merely a *state of existing,* to a *state of optimum health.*

To capitalize on your body's ability for optimum health, you must move out of a narrow way of thinking to see the benefits of alternative and preventative care. It requires proper exercise and nutrition, as well as utilizing alternatives such as chiropractic, or homeopathy. Herbalists, homeopaths, and naturopaths prescribe proper use of supplements in addition to their non-invasive techniques for diagnosis.

Many people who use alternative caregivers, are still operating from a remedial philosophy. For example, if they visit the chiropractor only when they are in pain, and quit as soon as there is no pain, that is a remedial approach. It overlooks the potential for restorative and preventative care.

The philosophy which recognizes the possibility of attaining an optimum state of well-being is different from the remedial approach because care is not related to symptoms. It is different from the preventative philosophy, because it is centered in the present. It is not about doing something *in case of something* that *might happen* in the future. It is about being the best you can be today! When you are the best you can be every day, you will be the best you can be in the long term - that is optimum health.

Time out:

What does wellness mean to you? What are some of the habits you need to change to increase your potential for optimum wellness? Does your health care plan include alternative therapies?

Fitness

Increasing awareness of the benefits of physical fitness is becoming wide spread. The changes brought by automation have increased the need for aerobic exercise. How you fulfil the need for aerobic exercise is a personal choice. There is an abundance of choices, from organized sports teams to fitness facilities, cycling, walking, and running. Your choice needs to be influenced by the condition of your overall health and what interests you!

Consultation with your medical doctor should precede any sudden changes. You need to be sure that you have no undetected health concerns which would affect your ability to participate in the regime of your choice. Whatever you choose, the needs of your physical self should be a part of your written Action Plan. Remember that it is a long term commitment. By living today in the way you want your future to reflect, you begin to create a future that fulfils your intentions and aspirations.

Time out:
Do you have a written fitness plan? What do you do for exercise?

Nutrition

Our bodies are able to maintain themselves in perfect balance if they are provided with the nutrients they need. Unfortunately, we have conditioned ourselves to believe we need all kinds of foods that are unnatural.

We eat fruits and vegetables that are picked under-ripe and stored for extended periods of time. This depletes the food of its natural vitamins. Food processing companies add synthetic vitamins to replace the natural vitamins lost during processing. Additionally, we consume additives, preservatives, and chemically altered foods.

We attach meanings to food that are not related to our physical needs. Food

> *"Worry kills man, fear kills man, hate kills man, jealousy kills man. Man doesn't do these things with his intellect; he worries, fears, hates, and is jealous with his organs. Man is a mechanism run by electricity, a machine made up of twenty-eight trillion electrical cells. Electricity keeps the flame of life burning in the cell. In a hate jag or a fear or jealously drunk you destroy an irreplaceable part of yourself."*
>
> *- George Crile, M.D.*

has become: a symbol of celebration of good times; an indicator of financial status; a measurement of sophistication. Healthy physiques have been ignored, as society has adopted the ideal of the extremely thin female body. This has added to the interpretations some people attach to food.

Some, who choose to rebel against the societal ideals regarding weight, exercise the personal right to "eat as they wish." Eating to excess may become a weapon, in a misdirected fight against authority figures and against standards imposed on them by others. The result is obesity, and a further detachment from their innate ability to select foods appropriately.

Abuse of food leads to an inability to sense the difference between hunger and other cues that activate the urge to eat. The more closely we listen to our bodies, the more clearly we will understand what to eat and what not to eat. It takes a lot of re-conditioning, however, I believe our innate intelligence can guide us away from fat and sugar to choose a high fibre, natural diet. Changing our beliefs surrounding food and becoming tuned in to our bodies' natural rhythms requires us to re-nurture ourselves. It requires changes in our conditioned responses and doesn't bring results overnight.

Relaxation

The fast paced lifestyles most of us have adopted, are not conducive to relaxation. When we fail to relax, stress builds to unnatural proportions. Accumulated stress is a killer. Stress can lead to headaches, back aches, high blood pressure, digestive disturbances, and even heart attacks. Here again is one of the places where many people

> *"It is not the facts and events that upset man, but the view he takes of them."*
>
> *- Epictetus*

cover up symptoms rather than dealing appropriately with the source of the problem.

Often, we lease out our head space to unworthy tenants. Thinking constantly about things we cannot change, or giving time to irrational thinking causes mental overload and interferes with normal functioning. Stress is often caused by the perception of the situation and not from the situation itself. Here is a step by step strategy for changing your perception.

- Stop.
- Look at the situation from a different perspective.
- Ask yourself: "Am I living in present centered awareness"?
- Ask yourself: "Am I unencumbered, free from past experience paralysis and future enchantments"?
- Ask yourself: "Are irrational beliefs or fears hindering me from reaching my full potential"?
- Alter the perception of the stress causing stimuli to neutralize the effect of the incident.
- Determine how you can respond differently.

Learning stress manangement skills can be like moving to a house with larger closets. It takes no time at all for the larger closets to fill up. Likewise, we tend to keep ourselves stressed to our maximum. Learning to reduce our exposure to stress is most beneficial.

Every day, allow yourself ten minutes of total silence for relaxation. Meditate to bring harmony between your physical and spiritual sides. Take time for leisure! Leave your work behind when you are not at work and when you are on holidays. Remember to take at least one holiday every year. It doesn't have to be a luxury cruise. It does need to be away from home, a break from familiar routine. When you return you will have a new outlook.

Your physical well-being is very important. Other aspects of your life are hard to enjoy if you have lost your health. Most health problems are caused by an unwillingness to make the changes you know you need to improve your lifestyle.

Look beyond the realm of your personal health reality to find your optimum potential. Strive to be the best that you can be, not merely allowing yourself to be content with just getting by. Physical well-being is a lifelong commitment. It requires consistent, and continual attention. Like all other areas of your life, you have an individual responsibility. Be proactive. Have a plan and review your plan often.

Time out:

Do you need to relax more often? What do you do to ensure you get proper nutrition?

Chapter 11

Operation Excellence

> *"Where there is no vision the people perish..."*
>
> *Proverbs 28:18*

Defining Your Vision

It is a nightmare when your dinner guests arrive hours after you have cooked the meal. I once had guests who arrived three hours late for dinner. When they finally arrived, they were arguing. The wife stated they had been lost for hours. The husband argued he knew that he was at the waterfront; and that he knew he needed to get up the mountain. He said, "I was not lost, and I knew where I was and where I was going." He said he just didn't know how to get up the mountain. Naturally, the wife was angry that he had not stopped to ask for help. There are times when we need to ask for help.

Attending workshops, getting personal coaching, and reading books are worthwhile ways of finding help. It is not a sign of weakness, but an indication of willingness to take personal responsibility for making your life more meaningful.

Additional information is often needed to assist in the planning process. Once we have the information, we need to determine which parts are useful to our personal plan. After determining this we can build an action plan (the Life and Career Plan). Growth depends on:

- Awareness of new opportunities
- Periodic revision of the Action Plan
- Continual implementation of the plan

These processes need to occur simultaneously, produce synergy, make the process of change almost effortless.

The Vision Statement of a business defines the objectives of the organization. The Mission Statement or a Statement of Purpose defines how the objectives will be achieved. A similar process is beneficial in developing our Life and Career Plan.

Suspending logic, at least temporarily, allows us to develop unobstructed visions. It is looking beyond the present to the future and imagining it as the ultimate fulfilment of your aspirations and intentions. It will not make any difference to our lives unless we also define how it will be achieved, and then act on the plan.

Before putting your vision into words, try to see it in the minds eye, draw it or depict it in some visual format. Use your imagination to see the unlimited possibilities. Developing a collage, by cutting pictures from magazines and creating a poster, may enable you to depict your aspirations and intentions.

Define your product or service, target market, financial picture, commitment to family, friends and community; depict leisure time, your ideal living arrangements and setting. Sometimes it is easiest to think from the end backwards. What do you want to accomplish by the end of the next year or by the end of your lifetime?

Imagine writing your own epitaph. What would you like others to remember about you once you are physically gone? Visioning is an attitude, based on a leap of faith. The vision becomes a reality when we believe we can achieve whatever we perceive.

Your first draft may require several revisions. That is all right, and is not necessary for it to be perfect. Remember that perfection, if it even exists, would be a state of total boredom, where all possibilities for improvement have been used.

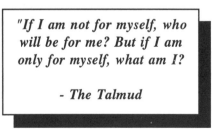

"If I am not for myself, who will be for me? But if I am only for myself, what am I?

- The Talmud

Purposeful actions will translate the vision into a reality. The dictionary defines a mission as "sending or being sent on some special work or errand." Your personal Mission Statement will stipulate what you stand for, and will bring you into accountability with yourself and others as you take action to initiate changes. It should be achievable, yet challenging enough to push you beyond mediocrity to excellence.

Action Plan

An Action Plan details the objectives and activities necessary to make the vision a reality. It is necessary to have a clear understanding of what you wish to accomplish in your lifetime, or the big picture, first. Then, ask "what steps are necessary to make the big picture a reality?"

Formulating an Action Plan, or Life and Career Plan, is a continuous activity. It needs frequent review and revision. If it is written and then left on a shelf, it stagnates and dies. Passion and action are the life-blood of the plan.

The steps which will assist you in creating the big picture should be measurable, manageable and well defined. They should be challenging enough to ensure against boredom, and realistic enough to prevent us from becoming overwhelmed. There needs to be clear milestones for determining your progress.

> *"It is not the strength but the duration of great sentiments that makes great men."*
>
> *- Friedrich Wilhiem Nietzche*

We have all encountered a staircase where each step was only four or six inches (10-15 cms.). It feels frustrating and awkward because our normal stride doesn't match the steps. Similarly, we have encountered stairs that were particularly steep. These are equally awkward. Not only do they not match our normal stride, we fear that we may fall. When we develop our Action Plan, the steps need to empower us in our ascent. Awkward steps hinder us, by causing a fear of falling or by causing a sense of frustration.

Guarantees

Part of the business plan articulates a company's guarantees. In our personal plan the guarantees apply to our commitments to ourselves and our dealings with others. It is doing what we say we are going to do. For example, we could plan to clear off all our miscellaneous debts and credit card balances within six months. If we fail to accomplish this we could promise ourselves that we are going to attend a workshop on personal money management.

Marketable Skills

Marketing is a process, and the sale is the last step in that process. Unless we are successful in making the connection between what is meaningful to us and what is meaningful to others, we will find ourselves without an income. Although happiness is not a commodity which can be purchased, the lack of money can cause unhappiness.

If you have mastered the skill of initiating changes, you will be quicker in responding to changes in the target market. It needs to be broad or diverse enough to protect you from being squeezed out. Delivering something that is of value to others translates into a measure of security. Capitalizing on individuality can enable you to identify a specific niche market. Life is worth living well. Your reality is only as limited as your thinking. Those who achieve the greatest accomplishments in life, learn the fine art of harmonizing their efforts with the efforts of others.

Time out:
What is your market niche? Who are your alliances?

Dealing with Competing Influences

Yes, competition can come from someone who offers a 'better' gizmo for less than the supplies cost to manufacture your gizmo. *Yes,* it can be the same product at the same price across the street in a newer store. But, don't be fooled. Not all competition comes in that form.

In private life, influences that compete against our aspirations and intentions will appear from time to time. They will also arise within the family, the community, on the job, and within ourselves - and in the physical, emotional, and spiritual aspects of our lives.

> *"That which does not kill me makes me stronger."*
>
> *- Victor Frankl*

Yes, it's sad but true, there will be co-workers, friends and/or relatives who feel threatened by our new found freedom. They will see it as a multitude of things which it is not. Some will say we have "gone insane." Some will say that "you must be involved in an affair" or that you "must be having a mid-life crisis." Some will imply that "it is just a craze, and sooner or later you will chill out." They will rationalize our behavior, read things into our behavior, and they will criticize our actions. They may even try to talk us out of any change we initiate.

Most often this happens because they are stuck and do not want to be confronted by anything that causes them to consider their own situation. Witnessing change makes them realize they too should be taking control of the helm, instead of floating downstream into the cesspool of indifference and destruction. These people remain in their state of misery because they are paralyzed with fear.

Acknowledge the strengths of these people, and demonstrate the clarity you have about your own actions. Thanking them for noticing that you are making changes, can be disarming. Be proactive rather than reactive - they are expecting you to react. When they don't get the reaction they expect, they find themselves out of their comfort zone and they are likely to retreat.

There are going to be times when you compete against yourself. The voice of your ego will attempt to tell you that it can't be done or that it is not worth the effort. You may be focussing on the worst case scenario. Your interpretation of the situation may be unrealistic and you may need a reality check.

When my daughter was four years old, she would go around the house singing, "I'm so happy, my mommy is going to die." She would sing this one line over and over. It was very disturbing that she found her prediction of my demise to be a happy thought. Explaining why it wasn't a nice thing to sing seemed to be of no avail. I knew she understood about death, because her pet rabbit had died. I was beginning to thinking that my child was deeply disturbed, and that I should consult a child psychologist. Then I got the reality check.

I had a home based craft business. There were some things that I would try to do while she took her afternoon nap. But on this day, she wasn't sleepy. After I got all my supplies out, she emerged from her bedroom. I was using dyes to create a wide range of colors. She came up to me, started to jump up and down and sing "Oh, I'm so happy, cause my mommy is goin' to dye right now."

Most barriers are merely illusions which we have accepted as reality. Having clear, measurable ways of telling when we are drifting off course or getting stuck, can enable us to stay focused on our vision.

Your Action Plan must outline a clear strategy for dealing with the competing influences you may encounter. Plan regular self-evaluations to determine if you are sabotaging your own growth.

Image

What do others perceive when they observe us? Sometimes we attempt to manage the impression others have of us by creating illusions. The image may be inaccurate if you are creating a facade. A facade is erected purposely, intended to be longterm and designed to deceive the viewer. It may create an illusion for others, but it does not change the real situation.

If the image we portray is distorted like the reflection in a pond, is the distortion caused by the murkiness of the water? Are we putting a smoke screen between ourselves and others? Is the image we are projecting a mirage, that when people reach it, they find it has disappeared?

We need to be aware of the image we are projecting. Mirroring actions back and imagining how we would perceive the behavior if we were the other person is effective. However, it must be done with honesty.

Operational Planning

My daughter showed early signs of being a pragmatist. I had brought a fishing rod home for her older brother. Like any four year old, she asked the typical "what's that?" and "how does it work?" questions. I diligently explained.

The next day, she came to me and said, "Mommy if you want a fish you take one of them sticks and sit by the river forever and forever and forever, right? But if you need a fish, you go to the store, right, mommy?"

It is the same when we plan our lives. There are a number of ways to reach the goal. We can do it the hard way if we have lots of time and enjoy doing it that way. That is our choice. It is important to remember it is a choice. We can spear the fish, use a fishing rod, use a large fishing boat and a net.

If we like fish but don't enjoy fishing, we earn money in other ways, and go to the store. The number of fish we have at the end of the day depends on many factors.

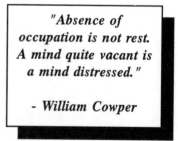

"Absence of occupation is not rest. A mind quite vacant is a mind distressed."

- William Cowper

Similarly, availing ourselves of the best resources and doing things in ways that are meaningful to us as individuals is crucial. Planning for success is no accident.

An operational plan provides the guidelines for conducting business. It assists management in making decisions, setting priorities, preventing or solving problems, and in the day to day operations of the business. The operational plan is referred to frequently. It usually contains long range goals, short range goals, followed by strategies and then work plans based on the strategies. Everyone in the organization needs to be clear about his or her role.

If we live without a written plan, it is easy to frequently change our minds about our priorities or our goals. While our personal plan includes our relationships with others, it is primarily a personal document. It should not be so limiting that it does not allow for additional information to be added. When it is written, it enables us to determine if new ideas fulfil the intentions and aspirations, that we have expressed. It is better to abandon any goal that would take us off track. If it is consistent with our intentions and aspirations then we can incorporate it into our plan. We should be readily able to see where it fits.

We choose to actively create a meaningful reality or to be a victim to the juxtaposition of the events of the universe. We become what we are by choice not by chance. Choosing to do less, which sometimes seems like the easiest, often leads to the most difficult experiences.

Risk Management

Every business person knows there are risks involved in operating a business. The quickest way to go bankrupt is to ignore the signs warning about danger zones. An attitude of "it can't happen to me" just doesn't cut it. Sometimes danger can be avoided. However, many of the hazards must be accepted and dealt with by appropriate planning.

The wise business person knows the difference between necessary and unnecessary risks and acts accordingly. The business owner takes a calculated risk. All change and growth involves an element of danger, as we confront the unknown. And conversely, any attempt to maintain a state of non-change also means encountering hazards. Then the choice is, what risks are you willing to take, and how do you intend to approach the risks?

Often we fear the unknown. Understanding the consequences of a choice, will reduce the number of unknowns. If we choose to ignore fear and take a 'leap of faith,' we may be taking unnecessary chances. Taking risks that are too large to manage and taking too many of them will lead us to emotional, physical and spiritual bankruptcy.

If the risk is too great, and perhaps unidentified or undefined, we will be forced to make instantaneous decisions in response to the outcome. This will not allow us time to think critically or creatively. Then the decisions made will be based mainly on emotions. If we are experiencing fear or anxiety at the time, it is not likely that the decision will be an acceptable one. Later, we will be faced with remorse, regret and maybe resentment. Not only are these emotions a barrier to further growth, the result of living this way affects your physical health. Ineffective risk management can result in extreme levels of stress. Prolonged or excessive exposure to stress results in physical and psychological illness.

Ignoring danger can result in traumatic events. Sometimes we can make choices which keep us in a state of anxiety for an extended period of time. Too much stress can lead to extreme fatigue, irritableness, "bingeing" or loss of appetite, and depression. Facing trauma may result in a total shutting down of emotional responses. The person can become emotionally numb, unable to respond to affection. Personal growth cannot co-exist with these conditions.

Stress can be controlled two ways: first, by controlling the risk factors and second, by controlling our reaction to situations and circumstances which induce stress. Defining the hazards in terms that can be measured, enables you to look at possible ways to reducing the number of unknowns. Look at change as a number of smaller steps, instead of one larger change. Dealing with smaller steps enables you to remain in control. A proactive plan reduces your reactionary responses to circumstances and situations. Actions which assure you that you are in control are reaffirming and lead to positive results.

In the area of personal change, that may mean having a support network - people who are willing to listen and understand without passing judgement. Often the resources which reduce the sense of danger are well within our reach. It is like making sure that you have a spare tire in your car before you drive somewhere. If we have the resources available to consult or utilize in the worst case scenario, we will be prepared and the risk will be significantly reduced.

Predicting the Future

We do not need a psychic to predict our future. Our actions are based on our internalized beliefs and are the physical manifestation of our thoughts and beliefs. We create our own reality.

Our future is easy to predict based on our past. If we continue to live our lives the same way as we have been living them, we will just create more of the same. It takes a lot of effort to change the future outcome of our lives. Abraham Lincoln became president of the United States, only after repeated failures to succeed in politics. He did not become president because of fate, chance, or good fortune. How many of us quit, rather than persevere? Success comes from a consistently applied plan of action.

Business people always use the financial statements from previous years to forecast future sales and growth. When we actually stop and evaluate where our present course of action is taking us, it provides two valuable assets. First, we will discover whether we are making progress and just need to add more skills to increase growth, or it provides the shocking reality that we are on the way to mental, physical or emotional bankruptcy. Second, it provides a guideline for present and future plans and a measuring tool for determining progress. It is very hard to change the outcome of your life, if you do not understand what contributes to your reality. Separate the factors that are a liability to your progress from the factors that are an asset to your progress.

However, behavioral change is profoundly difficult if it is not preceded by changes in beliefs and attitudes. What we believe we can achieve, is never exceeded. We need to aim high. What would happen if an athlete said, "My best time was eight minutes. If I manage to do the same distance in ten minutes I will be satisfied"? Any goal we have personally already surpassed cannot continue to be a goal. Growth depends on increasing the challenges of life, not shrinking away from them.

Having determined the results of our past actions is the first step in predicting our future. The second step is to determine what actions we need to take charge of the future. In order to accomplish this, it is necessary to change debilitating beliefs and create an action plan. Once the Action Plan is created, and a commitment is made to carry out the Action Plan, then it is possible to adjust predictions of our future, based on the new information. The accuracy of our predictions depends on our honesty in assessing the past, and our commitment to our Action Plan.

Not Without a Price

Growth has a price. Change has a price. Attempting to avoid change has a price. The choice is yours. You need to decide what you are willing to invest in. The results of avoiding change can be feelings of frustration, disappointment,

> *"A man's life may stagnate as literally as water may stagnate, and just as motion and direction are the remedy for one, so purpose and activity are the remedy for the other."*
>
> *- John Burroughs*

depression, victimization, and loss of self-worth. That is a hefty price. It leads to mediocrity or maybe even to stagnation. Making this choice can lead to an existence, but never to an energized, revitalized, vibrant lifestyle.

Growing pains can hurt. The loss experienced with change can be painful. Nevertheless, the end result can be well worth it. If we are in control, and if it is something we want - **it is** worth it. If you have any doubt, then you have not reached far enough down into your inner self to discover your passion. Once passion is the motivator, no pain is too great.

Letters of Intent

Letters of Intent are used by people starting a business or within existing businesses when they are seeking funds from a financial institution. A letter of intent is a letter from another company, or an individual, stating that they intend to use the services or products marketed by the company.

Power is *the ability to do or ac*t and power is not *control over anyone or anything*. Following through on our intentions is a powerful behavior because it proves our credibility. Others are not afraid to trust us if they know that we will follow through on our intentions. When smaller commitments are made and kept, it becomes easier to negotiate larger commitments.

For the purpose of Life and Career planning, we can use Letters of Intent to clarify and reinforce our personal commitments between ourselves and significant others. A letter from a partner, clarifying the intentions to play a particular role in assisting his or her plan could be a mutual tool for growth. This is a symbolic way of reaffirming our commitment.

Time out:
Take the time to put some of your intentions in a letter to significant others in your life.

A Journey Worth Recording

Keeping a journal is a therapeutic activity, and is widely accepted in the counselling community as a tool for self-discovery and healing. Journalling is the act of keeping track of your life on a daily basis. While there are a number of approaches you could take to journalling, I recommend using a *feeling* journal. More personal growth is experienced when we write from the point of feeling, than when the journal is merely a chronological objective list of events.

For the journal to be an effective tool, your writing needs to be spontaneous and unedited. The strongest feelings are the first ones to come out. Later you can read back and see how your feelings affected your problem solving strategies. The main thing is for the account you write to be unedited and honest.

Some people have a fear of their journal being read by others. If this fear arises, the benefit of the journal is reduced. Be honest with yourself; you cannot do this as long as you are afraid of the journal being found. There is definitely an issue of control that needs to be addressed if you feel that you have a lack of privacy. Your journal is a personal possession it must be respected by others in the household. These factors affect the value of your journal:

- The consistency with which you write in it
- The honesty with which you write
- The depth of feelings you are willing to expose
- How often you refer to it in the future

When we consistently deceive ourselves, we erode our self-esteem. We love ourselves conditionally, based on a number of distorted or false pieces of information. When we learn to love ourselves unconditionally, we no longer have any reasons for trying to hide from ourselves.

It is necessary to be able to experience feelings and act appropriately when our feelings make us uncomfortable. Any action we take toward others, based on our feelings, is inappropriate if it causes others to be hurt, emotionally or physically. If you have a tendency to act aggressively when you are angry or hurt, you are confusing your own feelings with other people. Even if it may seem the other person was involved, you make the choice about how you are going to feel. The important thing is that you learn to understand why and when you experience certain emotions.

Use your journal as a tool for self-discovery. You can learn to deal more effectively with experiences by learning what worked or did not work in the past. You can brainstorm for new ways of dealing with things based on the information you have.

Maintaining your Halo

Many religions have symbolized saintliness using a light disk or radiance around the head of a divine or sacred person in a picture. This is often called a halo. This halo could be compared to the energy others feel from being around us when we are living well.

When we have sheer enthusiasm for life, a positive attitude, a strong belief in self, and unconditional love for others, we extrude an energy which others can feel. It starts from a point of self-realization, self-appreciation, healthy self-esteem and an overwhelming love for life.

The feeling of being really in tune with life and the environment, is the best feeling a person can experience. The only way of getting that feeling is through doing enough self-examination and self-work to overcome the barriers which keep us in a state of mediocrity.

Once a person experiences the feeling of harmony, the desire to see others experience it for themselves is overwhelming. Harmony occurs when our beliefs and values are synchronized with our actions. This moves a person from *a state of being* to *a state of giving*. Projecting enthusiasm for life, and giving to others, produces more energy. It is like exercise.

However often, and however strong the field of positive energy we emit, we have the ability to increase that energy. Understanding our personal value to others, and accepting praise when praise is due, is a resource which can help us grow.

We may receive a thank-you letter, or some type of letter of recommendation, and view it as only a formality. We are quick to toss the letter in the circular file, because we fail to value it. These letters are not trivial. They are important documentation supporting your future growth. Your collection of letters is your Halo File. It is a file full of reasons why you should consider yourself to be a *saint* or extraordinary person.

Refer to your Halo File when you are going through a difficult experience. Reviewing the letters can help you regain a positive perspective.

Sometimes, people assume that there is such a thing as having too much self-esteem. This erroneous belief comes from observing a person who has pride, (the kind that makes them think they are better than others) or conceit, (which is a fanciful illusion of one's accomplishments). Pride and conceit are not synonymous with self-esteem. Pride and conceit are motivated by competition, and one-up-manship. Self-esteem is the secure feeling people experience when they accept themselves. It is the opposite of self-doubt. A healthy regard for our personal achievements, and a belief in oneself leads to self-confidence. Start a Halo File and remember to wear your halo and polish it often.

Time out:
Do you have letters, certificates and other mementos that need to be part of your Halo File?

Things that Matter

In a business plan, supporting material includes documentation verifying your abilities to carry out the proposed business. In your personal plan this may include a resume, certificates, diplomas, membership in business associations and other similar papers. Other papers that may be relevant are copies of: land titles, legal agreements, pre-nuptial agreements, marriage licences, transcripts, diplomas, degrees, citizenship papers, letters of thanks, awards, scholarships and other pertinent information. Do not underestimate the value of acknowledgements for smaller achievements.

Each accomplishment, large or small, may serve as part of the functional or creative path which leads us from one place to another. It is a choice that separates those who are really living, from the living dead - who merely exist. Life is a process. It is a sad existence for those who live it in expectation of that elusive *some day* when things are going to be just right, so they can start to enjoy life.

Therefore, a proactive approach is to gather supporting materials. These are the gemstones that will enable you to complete the mosaic of your life. They represent your creativity, talents, interests, skills, knowledge and personality. Then, continue to build the mosaic incorporating new gems. As you move forward to activate your Action Plan, you will add to your work of art.

Discard the stones that will take away from the mosaic you are creating. Chisel the pieces that need a little work. Polish some of the gems, if that is going to make them more beautiful in your masterpiece. As the master craftsman of the project, you can choose how you want the finished product to look. It is always necessary to allow time for the process. Creating a mosaic takes many hours - weeks or even years.

Remember, life is a process, and you create its meaning. You create the future as you live each day. Remember to enjoy the abundance each day has to offer. Savor a few quiet moments each day. Live with balance. Welcome challenges and change. Most of all, enjoy the process.

"This is the true joy in life, the being used for a purpose recognized by yourself as a mighty one: being thoroughly worn out before you are thrown on the scrap heap; the being a force of nature instead of a feverish selfish little clod of ailments and grievances complaining that the world will not devote itself to making you happy."

(Man & Superman 1903)
- George Bernard Shaw

INDEX

What is Personal Success Coaching?

Personal Success Coaching is a 21st Century concept. A personal coach is a consultant who helps to get you on track, and keeps you on track. The client is guided through the process of discovering his or her passion, then the client is assisted in making it a reality in the most effortless way possible. It is about supporting and guiding individuals to clarity and achieving both their personal and professional goals. Like the sports coach, the Personal Success Coach teaches techniques, assigns exercises, identifies barriers to success and motivates.

While Personal Success Coaching is a concept that has just begun to catch on, it is the way of the future. The March 1997 issue of the Sounding Board (Vancouver Board of Trade) stated, "Instead of 'what is a coach?' the question for the next century may well be 'who is your coach'?"

Who needs this type of consulting service? Coaches work with people who are sales people, entrepreneurs, managers, CEO's, employees and students. Many clients are already successful in business, but have come to a point where they are concerned about the cost of that success to other parts of their lives. They assist busy clients in finding ways to restore balance to their lives. Approximately 80% of the service is done over the telephone, and via e-mail. This eliminates travelling time, and increases accessibility. It enable clients to work with the coach of their choice, regardless of where they are located.

Coaching provides the missing link between motivational speakers and the achievement of results. A person can attend an Excellence seminar and leave pumped up, yet often two weeks later, he or she may be right back in the same rut. Coaching consists of weekly sessions, usually half an hour to an hour long. Learning to live more effective and balanced lives is similar to becoming a professional athlete. It takes consistent practice, a readiness to acquire new techniques, and a clear focus.

About the Author - Kristi Nielsen

Education:

- Bachelor of Arts, Adult Education
- Instructors Diploma
- Life Skills Coaching Courses
- Small Business Development Certificate
- Toastmasters - ATM Bronze-97

Experience:

- Twenty years as small business consultant and coach
- Twenty years owning and operating home based, retail, manufacturing, and wholesale businesses
- Community Economic Development Advisor
- Instructor in career search, life skills, and small business start-up
- Currently practicing as a Personal Success Coach, professional speaker and workshop facilitator
- Member of (IFC) International Federation of Coaches

Professional Speaker:

- Kristi Nielsen is an accomplished speaker, and speaks to groups of 10 to 2000 people. She is currently a member of CAPS (Canadian Association of Professional Speakers) and a member of Toastmasters International.

Kristi Nielsen is available for speaking engagements and workshops. She is a Personal Success Coach and is available for individual coaching. She can be reached by e-mail at: action@dowco.com or by phoning 1-604-850-5757.

09/09/1997

Other professionals say about Kristi Nielsen:

- "I would describe Kristi as a person who has made it her life goal to inspire others to live with passion and to take control of their own lives. She will succeed with this goal because she has demonstrated this in her life. Ms. Nielsen has displayed many qualities as an educator and coach...her ability to work well in a team atmosphere...to work with a diverse group of people... to understand client needs while treating each with respect".

  Robert Barker - Employment Training Supervisor

- "Kristi strikes me as an individual with extremely high energy and drive. She is very articulate...she is able to see beyond mere information to the level of application and implication. Ms. Nielsen has chosen a career where she can educate, and be an advocate of other adults needing life skills, self-management skills and empowerment to get on with their own lives...Kristi will make a positive contribution in that field especially given her quick mind, her easy manner with others and her skills."

  Mark Hoffman B.Sc., CS, MA

- "Kristi is one of the most capable and inspiring people I have ever known...She is a gifted public speaker, a very good writer and a natural leader."

  Madeleine Hardin, MA